TRANSFORMATION

TRANSFORMATION

J.G. BENNETT

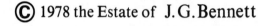

© 1978 the Estate of J.G. Bennett

Library of Congress Catalog Card Number: 78-60760
ISBN: 0-934254-04-4
Claymont Communications
Claymont Court, P.O. Box 926
Charles Town, West Virginia 25414

" *The very aim of our society seems to be to remove from people responsibility for their lives and acts. The way of transformation must be the exact opposite of this. Whatever else it may lead to, it must make us into free, responsible individuals, able to direct our own lives in accordance with the greatest objective good.* "

CONTENTS

One aspect of the book *Transformation* is Mr. Bennett's attempt to put into words the essence of the work and the process of self-creation. It is a strange process by which one lifts oneself or is lifted from one level to another. Each level is different and requires its own particular kind of work. Mr. Bennett's vision encompassed a practical situation in which an organization of human existence could take place harmoniously.

He established centres or schools for work on these lines. One such exists in the U.S. at Claymont Court near Charles Town, West Virginia. It comprises a "school for continuous education" and a place where the practical aspects of the work can not only be studied, but experienced by people at different stages, sometimes known as the philosophical, theoretical, and practical, and sometimes, as referred to by Mr. Gurdjieff, the exoteric, mesoteric, and esoteric.

Books are like maps, but there is also the necessity of travelling.

PREFACE

IN HIS OWN INTRODUCTION to this book the author mentions that twenty years have elapsed at the time of writing since his return to Gurdjieff in 1948. This puts the date of writing at around 1968, which conflicts with a scrawled 1963 on the typescript itself. The author was accustomed to be precise about such figures and other indications in the text tend to confirm the later date. Thus there is frequent mention of both the concluding volumes III and IV of his major work *The Dramatic Universe* as having been completed. These appeared in 1966 and 1967 respectively. A little reading between the lines produces at least one more clue, almost as definite as the first, for the attentive reader.

The point of this little piece of detective work is that it places the book squarely at a very significant moment in its author's life: at the completion of one phase and the beginning of another. He had in 1968 finally fulfilled his personal undertaking — in the text he calls it a 'whim' — to write a magnum opus which would attempt a synthesis of human knowledge. He had produced a complex and difficult work, in a form which he hoped and believed would be of value and use to future generations. He had absolutely no interest in writing a work which would create any kind of fashionable stir in the literary or scientific world, and the four volumes of *The Dramatic Universe* attracted little attention.

1

So that task was finished at last and he was seventy years old — an age which, for him, held a special significance and promise for the final course of his life.* There are many reasons to suppose that he began at that time to reflect seriously upon the course of his own previous life and the stages of his own self-transformation. He never tried to conceal the many mistakes and false starts he had made: he was emphatic that he had taken a quite unnecessarily long time to come to certain realizations, to reach certain stages. Yet he had been unusually fortunate in meeting and obtaining help from many remarkable men: Ouspensky, Gurdjieff, the Shivapuri Baba, to name but three.

He had just succeeded in clarifying for himself many subtle and difficult ideas about the nature of man and the possible transformation of human nature. He could see just how far he himself had come along the way of this transformation and, with the special freedom and intellectual clarity that come from the completion of a major creative work, he surely saw more deeply than ever before. From the evidence of this book it seems that he set himself to see what was really important in all that he had learnt, and to express it in a simple concrete way which would have an immediate impact.

He did find such a way, using the principle of the **tetrad** or four-term system which so interested Jung and others. His own researches had convinced him that there are four sources of action necessarily involved in any activity of transformation. This was a discovery expressing substantially the same insight as Aristotle came to in his maturity with the notion of four **aitiae**. In fact, Bennett's philosophical work bears much the

---

*cf. His autobiography, *Witness*, Turnstone Books, 1974, p. 78

same relation to Aristotle's as the *Mathnawi* of Rumi bears to Aesop's fables.*

Working with such multi-term systems presents special problems. It is hard to keep in contact with the actual situation concerned and at the same time to see how the elements of the system concerned are involved in its working. In the case of the tetrad we can illustrate the dilemma as applied to the simple actions of eating a meal. Everyone knows that a knife and fork, plate and mouth are generally involved in the action: these correspond to the four elements. But the important thing is the **food,** and getting it off the plate into the mouth. Lose sight of **that** and the exercise ceases to be useful and becomes absurd. Table manners are not hunger.

Our author did not lose sight of the essential rôles played by the four elements in the human transformation. He set himself to clarify what those rôles are by appeal to his own direct experience and in the first chapter of the book he succeeds magnificently. This chapter conveys, perhaps better expressed than anywhere else in his writings, the real character of the actions involved in 'work on oneself' and the most direct advice on how to carry it forward. The treatment of the action of **sacrifice** in particular seems somehow to say quite new things — cutting away at one stroke a mass of confused ideas and exposing the essential anatomy.

But we have already arrived at the book itself. It will be useful to consider what the author's aims were in

---

*This is sometimes expressed by the joke about the man coming to read Rumi having only read anything like it before in Aesop. His first comment is: "Who does this Rumi think he is — Aesop or somebody?"

---

writing it, what kind of conceptions he had of its purpose and function, and why it was never completed.

He was aiming, as always, very high. In the text he envisages the book as one which might be of real practical use to others like himself who found themselves embarked on the way of transformation. It draws freely upon his own experiences and what his deeper insight now shows him of their significance. It is a book in which he is trying to convey just those essential notions that he himself would have found valuable during his long years of searching. But in his conception of its function he had a very bold and radical idea: of perhaps trying to communicate the very techniques of transformation themselves.

It is because he realized that this last aim is impracticable through the written word that he abandoned the book after the first six chapters. Indeed, all tradition is against it. Devotional manuals such as the *Philokalia* describe techniques, but they are intended for use in situations where a spiritual director is available, as that famous book *Way of a Pilgrim* makes so clear. In an article he himself wrote in 1969, a translation of a Naqshibendi Sufi manual of just such techniques described as the *Tanwir al-Qulub*,* he said:

"The creation of mental images which is both transitive (tasvir) and intransitive (tasavvur) is often referred to, but the technique itself is evidently handed down by personal contact. It cannot be adequately described in words, probably because the transmission requires some kind of telepathic communication between

---

Sufi Spiritual Techniques, J. G. Bennett, Systematics Vol. 7 no. 3, Dec. 1969, p. 244 ff

teacher and pupil. The same applies to the **zikr** or meditation . . ."

One might ask why, if he knew this, he should attempt the undertaking at all. One answer is that he was not a man to shrink from attempting anything merely because someone had told him that it was impossible. He was accustomed to verify things for himself. He therefore began the book on the assumption that it might be possible for him at that time and place. He had special gifts as a communicator and was no doubt confident of receiving special help if the work was one he was destined to accomplish. It seems likely from the above quotation that by the following year he had realized that the task was impracticable. The single surviving typescript contains many references to later chapters which were never written, and it is these chapters which were to have contained accounts of the techniques of transformation. He makes it clear elsewhere that the contribution made by a teacher in communicating such spiritual exercises to a group is more than a mere oral transmission.*

The reader may next ask why — if the book is incomplete and fails to achieve the most important aim for which it was written — it should be published. The answer to this is that even in its incomplete form the book contains very much that is fresh and original. In fact one can say that it is full of insights and viewpoints that clarify many ideas and facts in new ways, ideas and facts which it is really important for those seeking their own transformation to know and understand. Some of the reminiscences have an almost brutal sense of factual truth, which the author might

---

*cf. **The Sevenfold Work**, J.G. Bennett, Claymont Communications, 1975, p. 94

well have toned down a little during the course of subsequent rewriting or revision. The lesser aims of the book **are** achieved, even by what remains.

Finally, the book has a certain special vigour about it. It starts off from the word go with an optimism and gusto which speak in their own way of the high hopes and great possibilities that might be accomplished through it. One can well imagine the freedom its author must have felt on beginning it after the years of painstakingly difficult writing of *The Dramatic Universe* which he had just completed. Much of the book maintains a candid, almost conversational tone which lends itself well to being read aloud — as was established during the 1976 Summer School at Sherborne, when readings from the manuscript were given for an hour or so every day. The impact of the book was considerable, and the verdict of those attending was that it was an important work and should if possible be published.

In the last years of his life the author initiated the 'Five Year Plan' of successive yearly courses at Sherborne House, by which he went some way towards preparing a nucleus of trained people able to pass on the techniques of transformation. Later the work continued at Claymont Court in the U.S.A. This book provides an admirable introduction for those who, feeling the need for some inner transformation, wish to acquire some idea of what it involves before committing themselves further.

Since the typescript was in the form of a first draft, a certain amount of editing proved necessary in order to correct typing errors, remove infelicities of expression and the like. Certain of the chapter-headings and sub-headings have been re-worded, and two paragraphs rearranged. Textual alterations have followed the principle of clarifying the author's intention wherever possible.

References in the text to chapters that were never written have either been deleted entirely or replaced by footnotes referring to relevant material in other of the author's published works. Quotations have been checked where possible and corrected where it seemed necessary, and some kind of standardisation has been attempted in the use of footnotes and italics.

Note to the Reader

Even though descriptions of exercises really requiring a teacher to impart them have been omitted from this book, certain suggestions are made from time to time of definite experiments to be carried out. You will gain very much from attempting to carry them out; nothing or worse than nothing at all from merely reading about them.

It is a mistake to take any assertions which may be made in a book of this kind as facts, without making at least some attempt to subject them to critical examination. One can sometimes construct useful exercises for oneself by asking oneself the question: "How could this statement be verified?"

It is equally important, at many places in the text, not only to attempt to assimilate what is being said but to make the effort also to find out what one's own ideas are, and on what they are based.

Do not be in too much of a hurry to get to the end of the book. Remember that much of what it contains is the distillation from almost fifty years of experience of life, and unusually varied experience at that. It is worth pondering over.

J.G.B. *"There are some things which you, Babaji, must be able to see from your vision which you cannot speak about. Even if you wanted to, you could not·tell us."*

S.B. *"I cannot. Words cannot reach this. Words cannot reach."*

J.G.B. *"Therefore, if we wish to know what you know, we have to come by the same path that you have come by."*

S.B. *"Experience alone will teach you — experience is beyond explanation."*

LONG PILGRIMAGE

INTRODUCTION

THIS BOOK IS ABOUT TRANSFORMATION, that is, the process by which a man can pass beyond the limitations of his own nature and become a 'New Man'. I shall assume, without attempting to produce the evidence that justifies the assumption, that we all have the urge to seek for this transformation and that it is just this urge that distinguishes man from the brutes. Many descriptions have been given in religious and non-religious terms of the changes in a man that transformation brings. I shall not start by discussing the end — if indeed there is an end, because I believe that transformation by its very nature once started is endless.

The purpose of this book is to describe various ways, that I myself have tried during the fifty years of my own searches. It will not claim to be an exhaustive treatise or method, because there are many that I have heard of but not tried and no doubt many more of which I am still ignorant. I have, however, been exceptionally fortunate, having met several men and women whose lives were evidences of transformation and having learned from them most of the techniques that I shall describe. I hope to avoid theoretical descriptions for which I can refer the reader to my earlier books. My aim is to share with others my own experience of what has helped me at different stages of my life; but I must start by warning the reader who may wish to make use of some of the methods I describe, that what works well for one may not be suitable for another. Another warning is that some methods should not be attempted without the advice and supervision of an expert. Finally, I must make the point that in my experience nothing is so liable to be misunderstood as the description of inner or psychological processes.

All these warnings and reservations might suggest that I have little confidence that the descriptions I shall give will prove useful. I can only say that many times in my life I would have been very thankful to be able to have such a book. So far as I know, there are no modern works that deal with the subject of transformation in general. There are plenty of books that give practical advice for improving one or another side of our nature, but this is not the same as transformation, which must apply to the whole man. In reality, man is such a complex being and all parts of him are so interdependent that one cannot change one part without affecting all the rest. This is one reason why attempts at self-directed transformation run into trouble. We must be prepared all our lives to go on learning about ourselves. It is not easy to do much more than scratch the surface of one's own ignorance.

Some are more keenly aware of the hope of transformation than others and they will eventually find the teaching and the method that they need. For such people this book may be useful as a record of a life spent in search and experimenting. It may help them to recognize the character of methods they may discover. Others are well aware that they need some form of discipline and some method or technique of self-improvement and yet be unable to accept unreservedly the conditions of any organization, church or school they may have met. Such people are tempted to try to go it alone. To such, I can only repeat the advice given by the Shivapuri Baba, a great sage whom I was privileged to meet in the Himalayas shortly before his death in 1963. "A man must examine himself and he must know himself well enough to decide if he has the strength, courage and persistence to rely upon himself alone. If he has, he can do without a teacher and regardless of what it will cost him, persevere in the search for Truth or Ultimate Reality. Very, very few souls can do this. A Buddha, a Ramana Maharshi may have the singleness of purpose that a solitary search demands. Those who feel themselves lacking must find themselves a teacher and place themselves under his direction. If they cannot even do that, they had best take to religion."

I hope that no one will regard the methods and techniques described in this book as a substitute for direction and teaching. There are some who know that they are not able to sacrifice everything to achieve transformation and are sensible enough to know that they had best not enter the deep waters without a guide and yet feel the need for techniques to overcome defects or to get them through difficult moments in their lives. I would be glad to think that such people may find help in these pages: but they must not hold me responsible if they decide to use a method without advice from some experienced person who can verify its appropriateness for their needs and correct any mistakes in its use.

There are certain exercises that can be used to give rapid and striking results and which are not harmful in themselves. I have omitted these where there is a danger of self-deception. One may imagine that one is making great progress, because one has striking psychic

11

experiences and appears to be developing psychic powers, whereas in reality one may be drawing upon reserves of energy accumulated over years of seemingly wasted effort: I have many times observed that this can lead to very sad reactions and even psychic disturbances that are hard to rectify.

These words of warning apply to no more than a small part of the process of transformation. Most of the techniques described can be used without fear of harm and are indeed likely to be beneficial for those who, without any lofty aim of transformation, feel the need to practise some form of self-discipline.

With few exceptions, the techniques described have been shown to me by teachers who specialized in the various methods and I have tested and tried them in my own experience. In several cases, I was able to learn only the first stages of a particular method, because to go further I would have been required to attach myself to a particular teacher, or at least settle for a long period of time in a foreign country, neglecting my family and other personal responsibilities. The one teacher whom I followed — as far as I was able and he would allow me — for a long period was Giorgios Giorgiades, generally known as "Mr. Gurdjieff" or by his own family and intimates as Yorgivanitch. I met him first in Turkey in 1920 and last saw him five days before he died on October 29th, 1949. His "System for the Harmonious Development of Man" is a magnificent achievement and no one who has tried seriously to follow it can doubt either its basic principles or the value of the techniques he taught. It has, however, two defects, one of which is adventitious and the other, I believe, essential. The first is the dependence upon teachers of the requisite experience and personal qualities. Such teachers take many years to form and not all are willing to take the responsibilities involved. It is more than fifty years since Gurdjieff first established in Moscow his Institute for the Harmonious Development of Man and during this time very few competent teachers of his method have made their appearance. The second defect is not so easy to formulate. In an obvious sense, one can say that Gurdjieff's method depended for its effectiveness upon his presence, so that when he died the driving force went out of it. It is probably truer to say that it depended upon the transmission of a particular energy or substance which Gurdjieff had in limited quantity, whereas it should be drawn from an inexhaustible source. I shall have to say a great deal about this substance, the reality of which is for me established beyond doubt. It has been compared to water which can be obtained from a river in buckets and carried laboriously to the plants that need to be watered. The same water can be obtained by an effort made once and for all by constructing an irrigation system. It can also come in the form of rain and dew. Without it plants cannot live. According to traditional beliefs, without it man's inner life and transformation must languish, and perhaps even perish. It would have been much easier to write this book and it might even have been taken seriously by psychologists and sociologists, if it had not been necessary to refer to this 'substance' — or perhaps more exactly 'these substances' — that play a vital part in the process of transformation. Unfortunately, I have been convinced that they are the key to understanding the process, and to describe techniques without referring to them is like describing a motor without explaining that it needs fuel to make it work.

This leads me to mention Subud, which is based on a technique known as the **latihan,** the action of which is produced by what is described as "the great life force". As I have written several books about Subud,* I will not describe it here in detail; but I must set down some conclusions reached after ten years' experience of its operation. For some reason that has not been made clear, Bapak Muhammed Subuh, the founder of Subud, has increasingly rejected the place of knowledge in the operation of the latihan and has insisted that it is due to the direct intervention of the Divine Will. For those who can believe this assertion, the effect is evident and powerful. It is not, however, necessary and many have responded to the latihan in spite of avowed disbelief in any kind of supernatural power.

There is no doubt that many people — perhaps several hundred scattered through thirty different countries — have really profited by the Subud latihan and have continued to do so for a number of years. It is equally certain that there have been disastrous experiences of mental illness and even suicide and many more cases where an initial response has been followed by prolonged inaction and final abandonment of the method. I am one of those who can say with confidence that I benefited greatly by the practice of the latihan over a period of about three years, after which it became evident that, for myself at any rate, it was not a complete and balanced technique. Moreover, I became convinced that the action was in fact due to a particular 'psychic energy' that could be transmitted from person to person and could not possibly be attributed to a supernatural action and still less to the

---

*cf. *Concerning Subud,* J. G. Bennett, Hodder & Stoughton, 1958.

direct intervention of the Divine Will, as Pak Subuh
had claimed.

Apart from the beneficial personal results that I
have described elsewhere, I owe to the latihan the
definite conviction that there are 'energies' that can be
transmitted from one person to another and that these
energies play a vital part in any process of transformation. I have met with them in a number of forms, and
will refer to them many times in the present book. I
have tried* to construct a theory of their nature and
operation, the basic ideas of which are derived from
Gurdjieff's teaching and that of the Sufis of Central
Asia. The main points are, first, that these energies do
exist and produce effects in this world. They are not
supernatural but natural; and second, that they are of
different kinds and can be blended and concentrated
and they can also be transferred and dispersed.

The defect of Subud, as it appears to me, is that the
assumption is made that the action of the latihan must
necessarily be beneficial because it is the direct operation of the Will of Almighty God. This assumption is
contradicted by innumerable facts and it is contrary to
all traditional teachings, which agree that only the
perfected man comes directly under the Divine Will.

The notion of a "Great Life Force" (in Indonesian
Daja Hidup Besar) is probably derived from the **Mana**
or Great Spirit beliefs of the Far Eastern people. The
Chinese **Tao** beliefs come from the same source. The
notions, usually regarded as 'primitive', of nature
powers have probably a firm foundation in reality.

When I first heard of Subud and asked the then
Indonesian Ambassador in London about it, he assured

The Dramatic Universe, Vol II Ch. 32 and *Energies;* Coombe Springs
Press, 1976 and 1964.

me that there were many 'wonder-workers' like Pak Subuh in Java and that they were greatly honoured by the people. I doubt if there are any others who have the same faith in Divine guidance and sense of a universal mission that has spread Subud all over the world in the short space of ten years and, what is more important, has communicated itself to many sincere and dedicated followers.

I wish I could have remained associated with the movement, which has so much to recommend it. My main reason for resigning as a Subud helper was simply that I could not agree with some of the vitally important claims made by Pak Subuh; particularly the claim that the practice of the latihan without attempting to understand its action was sufficient for the attainment of human perfection. At one time, I was ready to believe that this might be true; but, as I wrote in the last sentence of my book *Concerning Subud,* one can only judge such a claim by results, and the results over ten years have disproved it. It will be a splendid thing if the Subud latihan can be widely used as a means of opening the channels that connect the conscious and the supraconscious parts of man's nature, without requiring those who use it to belong to the Subud organization or Brotherhood.

'Not belonging' raises an important question. All who are interested in transformation are aware of the remarkable achievement of Krishnamurti, who for nearly forty years has gone up and down the world proclaiming that self-realization (which I call transformation) is possible without belonging to any organization and without any teacher or teaching. About 1932, Krishnamurti had several meetings with P. D. Ouspensky, whose classes I was then following, and Ouspensky used to tell us that he had never met so sincere or so persistent a questioner. He set us to try and answer Krishnaji's question, "Why a school? Why a teacher?" Ouspensky's own answer was that without knowledge we are helpless and knowledge can be obtained only from one who knows. I think now that the Shivapuri Baba's answer is more decisive: "If you find in yourself sufficient determination to put everything away except the search for Truth then go alone; if not you must find a teacher." I once expressed much the same view to Krishnamurti in a conversation nearly twenty years ago when I said: "You do not take enough account of the obvious fact that you have never been an ordinary man. What has been possible for you is simply not possible for others." But he would have none of it and insisted that every one is capable of making the effort. "Some will go more slowly than others because they are undecided, but all can do it, if they will only go about it in the right way."

It seemed to me, as it has to many, that Krishnamurti is a wonderful teacher who rejects the label of teacher and has an excellent technique which he refuses to call a technique. He has done a great work in arousing many thousands of people out of the stupor of modern life.

Having mentioned P. D. Ouspensky, I must say more about that remarkable man. He succeeded in convincing me and hundreds of others that by self-observation and 'work on oneself', it must be possible to 'wake up' and having woken up, to recognize and understand the true human situation. Though he is usually described as a pupil of Gurdjieff — even the chief pupil — he was in reality an original thinker whose personal convictions were radically different from those of Gurdjieff's teaching, from which he selected only those elements that coincided with his own beliefs. These beliefs were essentially pessimistic. This life is a prison, to which man must return again and again — not by way of reincarnation but by the repetition of the same life when and until he can achieve liberation. He was almost obsessed with the horror of existence. At an early age he had attempted suicide — an episode most movingly pictured in his autobiographical novel *The Strange Life of Ivan Osokin.*

Ouspensky was a marvellous exponent of Gurdjieff's ideas — and of his own personal beliefs, when he could be induced to speak of them. He was a deeply religious man who was in total revolt against religion as he had found it in his youth and in his subsequent search. It was as much as one's place was worth to mention the name of God at one of his meetings and his conception of the Absolute as almost — but not quite — infinitely remote from man seemed to account for all the godlessness of the world. He might have approved of the 'Death of God' theologies of our day and he certainly approved of Nietzsche, whose scheme of eternal recurrence he had developed in his own way.

Ouspensky clearly believed in the reality of mental substances or energies and described experiences of their operation in his communications with Gurdjieff. But he had a way of making every attainment seem remote, so that his pupils were afraid to mention experiences that confirmed the working of these energies, knowing well that he would drop on them like a ton of very cold bricks. The difference in his attitude towards simple religious faith and that of Gurdjieff

18

comes out strikingly if we compare their two books about the 'System': his own *In Search of the Miraculous* and Gurdjieff's *All and Everything*. Whereas Gurdjieff presents "Our all-loving Creator Endlessness" as directly concerned in the fate of mankind, Ouspensky asserts that the Absolute can know no more of the existence of all humanity than we men can know of that of a single atom or electron.

Ouspensky's negative attitude towards religion had a profound effect upon me and I did not begin to recover my religious faith until I returned to Gurdjieff in 1948. Only now, do I see how significant this was for me. I refer to it here to illustrate the difficulty in which any inexperienced and naive seeker is placed when he meets with someone whose knowledge and powers are clearly far beyond his own. Where the teacher does not ask for faith, but on the contrary demands that his pupils should accept nothing that they have not verified in their own experience, the temptation to take what one does verify in this way as a final truth is overwhelming.

To Ouspensky, I owe an abiding belief that remains with me to this day, that **to gain anything of value one must be prepared to pay for it;** though my understanding of what payment really means has changed profoundly. I gained a wrong notion of what is meant by 'super-effort'. Ouspensky's own example of walking twenty miles in a blizzard evoked the picture of an heroic action requiring one to drive oneself to the limit of endurance. This picture was painted on prepared canvas, for I had been brought up by my mother to believe that self-denial and self-driving were good in themselves. One must be on one's guard against regarding a particular teaching as right for oneself simply because one has been conditioned in childhood to think in that way. The immense debt I owe to my mother for her example and precept, that fixed in my mind that slothfulness destroys us and that tolerance is one of the best of virtues, far outweighs the disadvantage of having laboured for nearly sixty years under the illusion that the unpleasant is better for us than the pleasant.

The transformation of man is not something apart from his formation. The formative years of youth have an almost decisive influence on the rest of life. It can also be said that our 'formation', that is the training of our voluntary powers, should continue throughout combined with 'transformation', that is, with the development of those powers which are hidden from our ordinary sight.

This raises the question of two kinds of 'seeing'. Books about the hidden powers of man are full of references to the 'inner vision' or 'third eye'. We are accustomed to the term 'second sight' and its Latin form 'clairvoyance'. These notions refer to a real power that a few people acquire naturally without knowing how, but which most people could develop if they knew the way and were willing to take the trouble.

Here I must say that I failed for a long time to grasp the significance of the 'inner vision', in spite of having been taught by Gurdjieff many exercises that help it to develop. It was not until I went to Damascus in 1952 and met the Naqshibendi Sheikh Emin Chikhou that the importance of this kind of exercise began to dawn upon me. Other meetings with Sufis of the Naqshibendi order convinced me both that they had means of developing these powers and that several of them did in fact possess them. I myself was shown some of the simpler techniques and these in conjunction with what I had learnt from Gurdjieff convinced me that he must have learned much from the same source. I was, therefore, particularly interested to learn from Pak Subuh that his own teacher — whom he frequented from the age of 17 until he began to have the latihan experience at the age of 24 — had been the principal Naqshibendi Sheikh in the region of Semarang in Java. He has denied that he owes anything to this teacher; but it is evident that the language he uses and the descriptions he gives of the way man is made and works are all taken from the Naqshibendi Sufis. It seems likely, therefore, that without fully realizing it he has drawn upon this source, especially in his technique of 'testing' which is a kind of clairvoyant communication.

I mention this to emphasize the importance of forms of perception which do not depend on the five senses or the thinking brain. Many years ago, I heard that versatile philosopher C. E. M. Joad speak about the next step in the evolution of man, which he said would consist in the acquisition of the powers of telepathy and clairvoyance. These, he said, were already appearing sporadically in an unaccountable way in far more people than was the case a few centuries ago. He argued that the prodigious complexity of human societies of the future would lead to a complete breakdown of communication unless some such new powers were acquired by man. I could not help thinking that such powers could easily be abused, and that it is fortunate that in our society they cannot be acquired so easily.

This brings me to the next remarkable person from whom I learned some of the ideas and methods described in this book. In 1961, I visited in his forest retreat in the Himalayas the Shivapuri Baba, then by his own account 135 years old. I visited him again the following year, eight months before he died. I had heard of him thirty years earlier and some of my friends had visited him, but I had no expectation of seeing him myself until one of those unmistakable and yet unaccountable 'communications' came to me one evening and I knew that I would make the journey. A succession of apparently lucky chances made it possible. When I met him and said I had come in response to his summons, he waved it aside saying: "That is nothing but telepathy, it has no importance. Now, let me tell you about Right Living" and he went on without a pause-to explain his teaching.

Right Living or **Swadharma** in Sanskrit is the simplest imaginable way of life; but also when one grasps what it implies, the most demanding I have met. All ways lead to the conclusion that one can reach the goal only if one is prepared and able to make it the supreme and central aim of one's existence, sacrificing all that may stand in the way. No one put the uncompromising character of the choice more brutally than Jesus in the words "He that loveth father or mother more than me is not worthy of me . . ." But even such words as these may be interpreted as an attitude of mind, a decision to be made only when we are confronted with the choice between God and creature. The rest of one's life may not be greatly affected. The Shivapuri Baba insisted that the choice must be made **incessantly,** in small things no less than in great ones, and that it must be made in all three parts of our nature: body, soul and spirit. He therefore said that Right Living consists in three disciplines: one bodily and external, one mental and moral and one spiritual

22

— this last consisting in devoting oneself to meditation and the search for Ultimate Reality.

After my second visit, at his own suggestion, I gave three lectures in London on his life and work and invited those interested in his doctrine of Right Living to come and see me. Several came. I explained it to them as nearly as possible in his own words. Not one of them ever came again! The fault was mine, not theirs. No one who visited the Shivapuri Baba would willingly have missed an opportunity of hearing more from his lips. The reason why his words made so profound an impression of hope and confidence is that his hearers could not doubt that he had lived and was living the way of life he recommended. When he told us to: "Think of God alone — put every other thought out of your mind. It is difficult I know, but not impossible," what mattered was just that it **was** 'not impossible'. Difficulties and doubts seemed to vanish in his presence.

We must never under-estimate the importance of **darshan,** that is the visible presence of a very superior being. Such people are irreplaceable. The great majority of ordinary people lack confidence in the very possibility of transformation. When they are in the presence of a transformed man or woman, this confidence may flood into them and set them firmly on the path. This is sometimes called 'conversion' and the term is a good one, because it implies a radical change in the direction a life is taking. The change is not always permanent. It depends upon what the person concerned does about it. This book describes some of the means that one can employ to keep the process of transformation moving in the desired direction.

I have not mentioned in this introduction two factors that have become very important for me in recent years. One is the faith and practice of the Roman Catholic Church and the other is the action and the method of the Sufi tradition derived from the **Khwāja-gān,** or Masters of Wisdom, of Central Asia and introduced to the West by Sayed Idries Shah.

It might seem that I have fallen into the mistake condemned by Gurdjieff of taking "bits here and bits there" to make my own "Shachermacher-workshop-booth". I can only reply that for me personally there is a purposeful coherence in all that I have found over a period of nearly fifty years. I am convinced that seeming divergences and contradictions are really due to the inability to see deeply into the nature of man and his transformation. There is a wealth of valid teaching and sound technique scattered through innumerable schools, traditions, groups of various kinds as well as in the great and permanent organizations of religion. All this wealth forms a coherent whole, but its 'wholeness' cannot be recognised unless one can look deeper than the external forms.

We are, therefore, thrown back on the question: how are we to know what is to be trusted and what is right for us?

Can we select our own methods and use them as seems best to us, without risking some terrible mistake which an experienced friend or teacher might have helped us to avoid? If we need a teacher how are we to find him and recognize him? I shall try to give some kind of answer to these questions in the first chapter; but I must say that in the long run there is only one safeguard and that is our own power of **discrimination.**

" *The great teachers have said that success comes only to those who work. The help a teacher can give is dependent upon the readiness of the pupil to work and obey the instructions he is given. Without zealous work, the deeper meanings will never be found.* "

THE MASTERS OF WISDOM

Chapter One

THE FOUR SOURCES

TRANSFORMATION IS A PROCESS that must be started and kept going by various means. These means are of four kinds, each of which makes a necessary contribution to the right balance of the whole. If we neglect any of them or if we exaggerate and rely upon one to the exclusion of the others, the process will be thrown out of balance and we shall run into difficulties; we may even lose our way altogether.

We should look upon transformation as something that is happening here and now. It depends on what we **do,** and this in turn depends upon what moves and directs us. Each of the four means I am going to describe comes into our present moment from some **source** and that is why I have headed this chapter 'The Four Sources'. These are:

1. LEARNING

We start from a position of ignorance of ourselves, of our potentialities, of ways, means and methods and of the laws that govern the process of transformation. This ignorance must be remedied. We must search and we must learn. Before we can learn, we must learn **how** to learn. We must **wish** to learn and not expect to know without having learned. We may imagine that there is nothing we want more than to know the truth about ourselves and the world, but we show again and again by our behaviour that we simply close our minds to knowledge that does not suit us.

Even if we sincerely wish to learn, it still does not follow that we are willing to be taught. There is a story of a seeker after knowledge who asks a Sufi master to teach him and receives the answer: "If I am willing to teach you, are you willing to be taught?"

Some part of learning must come from ourselves. We must be willing to be sincere in our observation of our own inner states and hidden impulses as well as of our outward behaviour. But even sincere self-observation needs to be directed by knowledge of what to look for and how to verify what we think we have seen. How are we to learn?

Learning is an unending process — unless indeed there is an end-point in the Beatific Vision when we shall 'know even as we are known'. Perhaps the Beatific Vision is only the start of a new life when we shall begin to learn things that no tongue can utter. My own belief is that the ability to learn is so precious a quality that it cannot disappear from the perfected man. To be able to learn is to be young and whoever keeps the joy of learning fresh in him remains forever young. Everything that closes in us the channels through which new knowledge can enter makes it harder to escape from the prison of our own ignorance. The ignorant man is like a prisoner who languishes in his narrow cell, which will become his grave, because he has not learned that the door is not locked.

Ideally, we should learn from someone perfected in wisdom, who has passed along the way that we aspire to follow. We are scarcely likely to find such a teacher as long as we remain in a state of ignorance, nor should we be able to recognize him without experience on which to found our judgment. Many make the mistake of demanding a teacher for whom they are not prepared. This is strange, because no beginner in mathematics would demand to be taught by an Einstein or a Newton.

In former times, when travelling was difficult and books were few, the seeker had little choice. He had either to abandon everything and set out on a pilgrimage to places where teachers were reputed to exist or else to learn what he could from all the sources he could find. Nowadays, the situation has greatly changed. I was able to visit the Shivapuri Baba in Nepal after a flight of less than 24 hours from London. Fifty years ago the same journey would have taken two months. I receive every year dozens of books and pamphlets telling me about teachers and teachings all over the world. Anyone can go into a public library and ask for books about mysticism, yoga, sufism, zen and various techniques of self-realization, each of which usually claims unique authority and effectiveness. Lectures on these subjects are advertised weekly in all the great cities of the world. How is the seeker to choose? On whom is he to rely? This chapter is an attempt to answer that question.

Clearly one must learn from someone who knows. It is not hard to decide whether someone whom we might ask to teach us knows at least something of what we want to learn. Reading books is useful to give us a start; but, as I have already warned the reader, techniques can only to a very limited extent be learned from the written word. We can learn from books about the theory of transformation, but their chief value is in helping us to make up our minds whether transformation is possible or not; whether it is a fantasy or, if not a fantasy, a possibility so rare that you or I have no reasonable hope of achieving it.

Books can also help us to recognize the character of different ways. There are ways avowedly religious and others that are unattached to any particular faith. Some even profess no faith at all. Some are essentially devotional and of these some require personal devotion to one's own teacher. The seeker should be able to answer for himself the question whether he is able to devote himself in love and service to a particular person. If he cannot, he cannot expect to go far on a devotional path. Other ways require some specific form of asceticism, such as abstaining from animal food or from sexual intercourse, or practising severe or frequent fasting. Here again, the seeker should be able to measure not only his own strength but also his mental attitude. It is of little use to engage on an ascetic path to the rightness of which one cannot give mental assent. This does not apply to all paths, but only where the visible action required can be understood and tested. Those who are drawn towards a religious path may well find it right to accept what they cannot yet understand, or to obey orders against which their mind revolts. In other words, mental assent cannot be taken as a general rule for recognizing the rightness of a method. The reverse is also true. We may be wholly convinced in our minds that a certain course is both right and possible for us and only discover later that we have been led astray.

If we rely upon the advice of others, we may find that what suits their needs may not at all be right for us. If we ignore the experience of others, we may be in danger of choosing what appeals to our imagination, or even our vanity and self-love. If we decide to follow the crowd and use only such methods as are recommended by official 'experts', we shall find our scope lamentably restricted. Psychologists and pedagogues are concerned to remedy defects and to produce 'normal' people. This is admirable; but it is often true that the way to achieve normality is to set one's aim above 'mere' normality.

This book is written for those who wish to explore the possibility of transformation and who have already tried one or another method and remain dissatisfied. I shall try my best to be impartial, chiefly because impartiality is good in itself and by practising it I can hope to improve my own power of discrimination, which, as I wrote in the Introduction, is in the long run the only means by which we can distinguish right and wrong.

The study of the lives of men and women who are reputed to have been saints or sages, of books of wisdom and collections of wise counsels, all help to develop discrimination providing they are read with this aim in mind. It is even more useful to seek out wise and experienced people and use every device and artifice to draw them out and profit by what they have to say. Apart from such obvious steps, one should cultivate discrimination by forming the habit of suspending judgment on new ideas and people that we meet and yet not hesitating when we have seen enough to make a definite decision whether or not to pursue our contact with them more deeply. We should study good customs that have been followed for ages by different peoples and cultures and try to understand their real purpose. Such counsels as these may seem obvious and even trite, but the point is **to put them into practice.** Let the reader ask himself whether he is doing anything of a practical nature to improve his discrimination and judgment. He may find that he does the best he can to examine every important situation and take a right decision, but that it has not occurred to him that his 'best' might be improved.

I will suggest here a few rules that I have found useful and that may help towards 'right learning'.

1. Ask yourself whether what you are told or read can be verified. If so how? Verify before you accept.

2. If you have no means of verification, do not reject what you are told without first asking yourself whether it really matters to you if it is true or false.

3. If it really does matter, examine the source from which the knowledge comes and ask yourself if you are prepared to trust it until some means of verification turns up.

4. Never take anything you learn as final. Be prepared to look at it again.

5. Cross-checking is useful. It can give us confidence if we find that two bits of knowledge supplement and tend to confirm one another.

6. But remember that it is only possible to cross-check items expressed in the same language. We can get terribly confused if we try to compare one teaching with another unless we are sure that we know what both of them are trying to tell us.

7. Practise impartiality. Do not let 'like and dislike' influence your judgment.

8. Nevertheless, you must give full weight to your 'instinctive' reactions. They are often more penetrating than your thoughts.

9. Learning 'what' and learning 'how' are not the same and yet they can never be separated. We do not really 'know' something if we do not know how to make use of the knowledge. Knowing how — learning to 'go through the motions' — will not take us far unless we

know what we are doing. In other words, the distinction between theoretical and practical knowledge is only a matter of convenience. The two must always be blended if they are to give positive results.

10. Remember that all partial knowledge is precarious. Always try to see the whole to which an item of knowledge belongs. Even if you cannot succeed in seeing the whole, it is better to make the attempt than to remain with an isolated fragment.

11. Open your mind more and more.

12. Knowledge that is shared is better understood than knowledge which is hoarded. We can learn best by teaching; providing we never forget our own ignorance and remember that learning-teaching is a two-way process in which the teacher receives as much as the learner.

I shall deal in later chapters with the various things that we have to learn and how we learn them. Learning is the means of connecting ourselves with ourselves in the first place (self-knowledge), and with what is not ourselves, in the second (objective knowledge). Knowledge brings order and a sense of direction into our lives but of itself it does not transform us. For that, we must pass on to study the second Source.

2. STRUGGLE

We wish to change and be transformed, we wish to make our lives as full and as useful as possible and to find and realize our own destiny. All these wishes have their place in all of us; they are there because there is an **Ideal**. All religions and all teachings agree that there is an Ideal or Perfect Man. This perfection is not our own invention; the desire for it is part of our

33

nature. Children look for it in their parents. As they grow older the ideal becomes universal and objective. Even if they reject religion and refuse to associate the Ideal Man with God, the ideal still remains: we cannot live without it. The most distorted and horrible ideal is still for the man who longs for it his Ideal, and he must try to reach it whether he wishes or not.

We have all kinds of other wishes unconnected with the ideal. Even when we are pursuing it, we are incessantly distracted in body, feelings and mind. There is no stable unity in us that can wish always and in all states and conditions for the same thing. It is thus obvious to us all that we have in us a conflict of wishes. In the ordinary way, we shift from one wish to another according to what happens to attract our attention or according to the habits of behaviour we have formed.

So long as life goes on in this way the various impulses neutralize one another and we get nowhere, or rather we drift imperceptibly towards that gradual weakening of all wishes which is the mark of growing old. When all wishes are feeble, we drift towards death. This should be understood by everyone and probably is; but, not knowing what to do about it, most people close their minds to the situation and excuse themselves by blaming their circumstances.

And yet what is required is really very simple. **One must organize a struggle of desires or impulses.** We have some power of choice: not perhaps as free as we imagine and yet sufficient to organize the "struggle of 'yes and no'."

For example, everyone can find in himself or herself inner attitudes of mind and outer habits of behaviour that are contrary to their own Ideal. He can ask himself if he wishes to keep or to be free from one or other of these. Out of this self-questioning can come a decision to struggle with the attitude or habit he has examined. This simple example illustrates what is meant by struggle.

Struggle is possible because we men are not one indivisible whole. One part of us can struggle with another, but only on condition of being aware of **inward separation.** This can be experienced very simply in relation to our own bodies. We usually say 'I am tired' when it is obviously correct to say 'my body is tired'. Perhaps 'I' am not tired at all. If so, 'I' am separate from my body. I can then say to my body "you may be tired, but I want you to do so and so." A struggle may follow and out of the struggle my body may obey 'me'. The same kind of situation can arise in thousands of ways. Together these form the second great source from which the process of transformation is kept going.

Struggle with oneself can also be called self-discipline or 'work on oneself'. It can apply to body, feelings and mind, or to all three together. It can be on different levels of understanding and intensity. At this point, I am concerned only to explain the basic principle that **struggle depends upon our being conscious within ourselves of a separation of 'yes' and 'no'.** Only when we are conscious of this separation can we make an act of choice between the two.

Here it is useful to see that the choice must be specific and it must be absolute: "either this action or that action." There is no compromise. The doctrine of 'no-compromise' is easily misunderstood. It is often supposed that it is general and applicable to our entire lives. This is only true for those who have reached such a stage of transformation that the separation between the supreme wish for the perfect **Ideal** and all other wishes is clear and unmistakable in all circumstances. Only such people can make a complete act of choice. For ordinary people, there can be no question of a total commitment outside the immediate situation embraced by their consciousness of the conflict of desires. I call this immediate situation the **Present Moment.** Most of the time our present moment is so contracted that there is no room for separation and 'we' are **lost,** that is, our **will** is wholly taken up with the dominant impulse of the moment. In such a state, choice is an illusion. It is called **identification** or **attachment.**

In the state of identification we cannot struggle, because there is no one there to struggle. In order to struggle something must bring about in us the state of separation. Any kind of shock can do this. When it is a physical shock we call it 'noticing'. When it is a mental shock we call it 'awakening of attention'. When it is a moral shock we call it 'remorse of conscience'.

Obviously, not all struggle is for the sake of transformation. Whenever we have an **aim** to be attained and find that we are not doing what is needed we 'make an effort'. This effort is a struggle against some weak or rebellious part of our nature. Sometimes, we struggle to achieve unworthy or useless aims. In itself struggle is neither good nor bad, but it is bound to produce a result. Through struggle we grow stronger, by ceasing to struggle we grow weaker. If we can struggle with one desire, we shall find it easier to struggle with another.

Sometimes, people start on the way of transformation without any idea of what it means — simply because they do not like to be as they are. This dissatisfaction is itself a form of separation. Dissatisfaction, or awareness of being deprived of what one needs, is the force that prevents man from stagnating. What he does with this force depends upon what he understands. This is why knowledge must come in at the start of trans-formation. So long as we are dissatisfied and do not know what we really want, we shall probably do plenty of foolish things.

Self-knowledge and struggle with oneself go hand in hand. The link between them is discrimination. This can be expressed in the form of rules or 'guide-lines'.

1. Remember always that you can only struggle within your own present moment. Outside the moment of which you are conscious, there is plenty going on and you can know a good deal about it; but not struggle with it.

2. Organize your struggle: choose with what you will struggle and repeat the act as often as you become aware of the impulse you wish to struggle with.

3. Use discrimination. Do not be too ambitious. Learn to measure your own capacity.

4. Persistence will do what cannot be achieved by force. Drops of water wear away a stone: a cloudburst will leave it unchanged.

5. Don't be afraid of struggle. No one ever made themselves unhappy or injured themselves by struggle, unless they were over-ambitious, foolhardy or vain-glorious.

6. Remember that present struggle is the key to future happiness.

7. Do not chop and change. A very modest plan of action carried through to a conclusion can produce astonishing results.

8. Take decisions only when you are sure that you have both the intention and the ability to carry them out.

9. When in doubt of your ability, tell yourself that you will try your best. Then your 'best' must be your decision.

10. Never stop to regret failures or try to excuse them. They have gone out of your present moment, and there is nothing you can do about them.

11. Your body is ignorant; be just to it. Your feelings change; do not count on them. Your mind is volatile; do not expect that it can remain stable within your present moment. In short, be realistic about yourself.

12. Never forget that no one else can do your struggling for you.

I have dealt with struggle only in its obvious aspects that can be recognised by a beginner on the way of transformation. There is a deeper significance of struggle connected with energy. Struggle uses energy, but it also produces it. An unconscious struggle is always in progress in our organism: it is the struggle for survival which we share with all living things. When we fall ill, we become aware of this struggle and we must learn to adapt ourselves to it. Childbirth is a great struggle for life: the mother must give herself wholly to this natural obligation until it is over and she has recovered her strength. I mention these obvious situations to make sure that the reader understands that discrimination must always prevail. Foolish, indiscriminate struggle — as if it were an end in itself — leads to no good.

Struggle is the organization of the power of wish. Unless something in us wishes to struggle we cannot do so. The wish may be unconscious or semi-conscious, but by knowledge we can bring it into consciousness and so be able to organize it.

3. SACRIFICE

So far all is plain sailing. We all recognize at least part of what is meant by learning and struggling. Now we come to a source the very nature of which is to be hidden. A sacrifice that is seen to be a sacrifice is not a true sacrifice. We remember the counsels in the Sermon on the Mount. "Do not your alms before men to be seen of them", and of those who do so: "They have their reward." There is an obvious contradiction between this verse and the earlier one which says: "Let your light so shine before men that they may see your good works and glorify your Father which is in heaven." The contradiction disappears if one recognizes that the latter verse refers to struggle and effort, whereas the former refers to sacrifice and renunciation.

Before going further, I must try to answer two questions. Why is sacrifice necessary and how does it differ from struggle?

Sacrifice is necessary because **everything worth having must be paid for** and the word sacrifice is simply another word for payment, but as I will explain in a moment, it is not the same as purchase. Sacrifice and struggle work in opposite ways. When we struggle, separation comes first and choice or decision afterwards. In sacrifice we decide to separate ourselves from something that we are attached to. Sacrifice must not be a struggle: unless it is made as a free act of will, it is not a genuine sacrifice. Nor is it a sacrifice if it is made to gain some specific benefit. That is why I say that by sacrifice we pay and yet we do not buy anything. This is the secret, even the mystery of sacrifice. In one way it is not a mystery because to give expecting a return for what we give may be admirable, but it is not sacrifice. In another sense it is a very great mystery indeed, for it is a special kind of creative act that opens possibilities which cannot be opened in any other way.

To illustrate the mystery of sacrifice, let us take the simple example of 'giving way' in an argument when it is done by decision and not from weakness or fear. If two people are in opposition both claiming and believing that they are in the right, it is hard for either of them to give way unless they are compelled to by some stronger force. If either gives way unforced, because he chooses to sacrifice his pride or his 'face', the entire situation is transformed. The sacrifice creates possibilities which were not there before. The mystery of the act is that it appears externally to be a sign of weakness, and yet it proves to be the contrary. It invariably happens that the one who makes the sacrifice ends up with the advantage — providing always that he did not do it with this result in view.

Opportunities for sacrifice occur all the time, but their very nature is that they are not noticed. In the example I have cited, ninety-nine times out of a hundred neither adversary will notice the moment when it is right to give way. Another example is the anonymous gift. It is easy to give in this way with a feeling of personal satisfaction that one has avoided being thanked, but this personal satisfaction absorbs the possibilities of the act and it is therefore not a true sacrifice.

One must not make heavy weather of it. Sacrifice is an art that must be learned. Its operations are not obvious, but they are not beyond the scope of anyone who has once really grasped the principle.

The way I explain it to myself is based upon my idea of the Present Moment as the field of action of my will. If I decide to put something to which I am attached outside of my present moment, I form a connection that goes 'out of time'. That 'something', because I am attached to it, has become a part of myself: by separating myself from it, it becomes a channel through which new possibilities flow into my present moment.

I know that this is a difficult idea to grasp without a clear mental image of the way our present moment is constructed and I can only refer readers who wish to study this further to the fourth volume of my book *The Dramatic Universe.* * It is not necessary to grasp it for the purpose of this book. It is enough to realize that when I put away from me something that is precious, I create a special kind of force. I can feel this force acting on me and if I observe how it works a number of times, I shall begin to see for myself that what I have given up returns to me in another form and brings with it new possibilities.

The essence of sacrifice is **decision.** This is illustrated in the story of Abraham. God was satisfied with his decision to sacrifice his son and made with him the covenant which his descendents were to inherit. The merit of Abraham is usually taken to lie in his obedience, but this misses the point of the decision to separate himself from his beloved son. The situation is the type of all sacrifice and the ancient story is evidence of the wisdom that men had attained nearly four thousand years ago.

---

*cf The Dramatic Universe, Vol IV p. 13 ff.

It must be understood that the decision has to be authentic. One of Gurdjieff's Russian pupils tells this instructive story of his treatment of sacrifice. In 1918 at Essentuki in the Caucasus when life was very hard, he asked all the women of the party to give him their jewels. Mrs. H. had some family jewels that were not only valuable but her sole remaining material link with her past life. After an agonising period of hesitation, she took them to Gurdjieff and put them before him on the table and walked out of the room without a word spoken. When she was half way out of the house, he called her back and said: "I don't need these, you keep them". Several years later the story was told at the Prieuré and soon after Gurdjieff again announced that he was in difficulty and needed all the money they had. An American woman brought her jewellery and laid it on his table expecting to be called back, but he only said: "Thank you very much," and that was the last she saw of it. When she complained bitterly that she thought it was a 'test'; the others pointed out that even if it was a test, she had failed.

Not every genuine sacrifice is voluntary. Something may be removed from our present moment not by our own choice. If we are strongly attached — as for example when we lose a person near and very dear to us — we can respond by renunciation or by revolt. If we refuse to accept the separation and dwell upon our grief in self-pity or refusal of life, we lose the true connection, because we remain within our own present moment. If we accept the bereavement and renounce the impulse to brood over it and pity ourselves; the effect can be the same as that of a voluntary sacrifice. Indeed, the result may be extraordinary, for we can become conscious of a connection with another world 'outside' our own space and time.

I have insisted that when we make sacrifices we must not look for a return. This does not mean that there are no results or that one cannot recognise them. The fruit of sacrifice is **freedom**. Freedom is a very wonderful state of existence, for it is no less than **the possibility of a creative act**. True freedom is so rare in our human experience that few people can even recognize its taste. When we are free we are master of the present moment: we are not tied by the consequences of the past or controlled by influences outside ourselves. Freedom is almost the most precious thing in life: but the word has been so misused and so debased in its meaning that we take freedom to mean being without external constraints. The state of the world today gives the lie to any such definition of freedom. No one is free who is not inwardly free and this inner freedom comes in the moment of sacrifice. As our sacrifices are only partial sacrifices — that is involving the attachment of only a part of ourselves — the inner freedom we can get does not last long. But so long as it lasts it is unmistakable.

Sacrifice is never easy. Until the decision is taken it seems almost impossible. Not physically impossible but requiring an act of will that we refuse to make. Once a wealthy lady in one of Ouspensky's groups about 1923 said in the weekly meeting that she wanted at all costs to be free from herself and asked if she could do anything about it. Ouspensky asked her to name some possession to which she was particularly attached. "Yes," she said, "I have a Dresden tea set that belonged to my grandmother and is still intact." Ouspensky said: "Break one of the cups and you will know what it is like to be free." Next week she returned in tears and almost hysterical saying that she had tried a dozen times and could not bring herself to do it. Ouspensky's dry comment was: "So you see this desire for freedom is not worth one cup." His purpose was to show her what she could not do, not to make her ruin her tea-set.

Sacrifices must be made freely. They must not be beyond what we can bear. And they must be made again and again. The most valuable sacrifices are made when we give up inner attachments. Everyone is attached to his or her picture of himself. This picture usually includes 'being in the right'. Few can bear to admit that they are in the wrong. Every time a person who has this attachment to 'being in the right' is able to sacrifice it, he projects part of himself outside the present moment and this creates a state of freedom that lasts until it is dissipated by activity.

Here are some rules I have found useful in the practice of sacrifice.

1. Any desire for reward that creeps into sacrifice destroys its value.

2. Be intelligent in your choice of objects to sacrifice.

3. Do not sacrifice at the expense of others, unless you are able to make it up to them.

4. A half-hearted sacrifice is not much of a sacrifice.

5. Sacrifice what is precious to you in this present moment.

6. Never bargain over sacrifice.

7. Do not be fool-hardy and attempt sacrifices that you will regret.

8. Measure what you can bear. This is the measure of what you are.

9. Search yourself for attachments and ask yourself whether you are ready to sacrifice any of them.

10. Right sacrifice is made for a good reason, but not for a good result.

11. Keep your sacrifices hidden from others, or if this is impossible contrive to make it seem that you did well out of them.

12. Sacrifice must not be the result of struggle, but of decision. It is a decisive act that is made in a moment and there must be no hesitation or second thoughts once the decision is made.

Sacrifice is possible because man has free-will. It is likely — at least that is what I believe — that the only way in which free-will is exercised is in the act of sacrifice. When this act is made we have a period of freedom when what we do and what we are are one and the same. This disintegrates, but it leaves a trace behind and this trace grows until it becomes the heart of our True Self, that is our real "I".

There is very much more that could be written about sacrifice. Why, for example, is this idea so very ancient in man's life that it can be traced back in its external and ritual forms for tens of thousands of years? Why did it ever take these external forms? Why has its true character never been explained?

I must at least answer the question of whether sacrifice is a specifically religious act. The answer is that it is certainly not exclusively religious, nor is it even necessarily 'good', that is, moral. There is little doubt that sacrifice with early man was an essential part of magic. Its purpose was utilitarian: to assure success in hunting, to increase fertility, to bring favourable weather for the harvest, to avert disaster and so on. It is used for these purposes to this day.

There is the Faustian sacrifice in which a man sacrifices what is most precious to him, his soul, in order to acquire the power of creation. All kinds of magic involve some form of sacrifice: without genuine sacrifice, magic is empty. I think it is likely that there can be unconscious sacrifice where a man gives up something really precious to him to achieve some imaginary purpose and experiences a kind of ecstasy of self-torture in the process. I mention this to illustrate my view that sacrifice is an act of will of a particular kind — that is putting something precious out of one's own control — and not in the aim or quality of the act. These two — the aim and the quality — certainly determine the kind of result that will come, but they do not open the channel that leads out of our present moment.

Finally, I must mention what to most people would not appear to be a sacrifice at all and that is the sexual act between a man and his wife. The seed of man is a part of himself and it is a very precious part, because in the living cells of the spermatozoa and the ovum is concentrated the creative energy which can bring into existence a new life. This energy is liberated in the act and it goes out of the present moment that the man and woman are sharing. As most people are drawn into the sexual act by desire or habit and expect from it a particularly intense sensation of pleasure, it would seem to be very far from a sacrifice. This view misses the whole point of sexual union, which is the opportunity for complete sacrifice of self in order to give satisfaction to the other. When this sacrifice is made, the act is truly creative and brings with it freedom and creative power. When it is not made, sexual union is followed by a sense of emptiness and even disgust, often accompanied by a feeling of having been ill-treated by the partner. Here then we have an act the very nature of which is to be sacrificial and yet in the great majority of cases is emptied of its true significance. This is, no doubt, largely due to ignorance. There is scarcely any other department of human life more lamentably misunderstood than that of sexual intercourse. It is treated as a mystery that may not be spoken of except by poets and psychologists — that is, by those who may be creative, but are usually selfish; and those who may be unselfish but are seldom creative.

The opportunities for sacrifice arise constantly in the normal conduct of our lives. They do not all have to be taken, but they should be recognized and understood. The man who has learned the value of sacrifice — and the joy of it too — has gained access to one of the great secrets of life and of transformation.

4. HELP

If sacrifice consists in thrusting something precious out of the present moment; help consists in allowing something precious to enter. It may not be at all obvious, but the question whether or not transformation is possible without help is the key to the whole problem of human life. I do not mean the question whether help is useful, but whether it is indispensable. If help is not indispensable, then at least in principle we can change ourselves by an action that can be produced completely by our own will. This means that our present moment must contain something that would enable it to become radically different (unless it is radical it is not transformation) from what it now is.

Some people say that such radical change is possible, and that the 'something' that makes it possible is really nothing but luck. The human brain, they say, is so immensely complicated that hundreds of millions of combinations are being formed every minute. One of these combinations may be completely original and open up new possibilities, without any need for help from outside. The same kind of argument is used to reject the idea that any Great Intelligence is at work on any scale large or small. Life appeared on the earth, they say, because out of inconceivably numerous chemical reactions in the primitive ocean or atmosphere of the earth, a self-reproducing molecule could have arisen by sheer chance — good or bad luck as you choose to look at it!

On this argument, the entire atheistic and mechanistic philosophy of modern life is based and that is why I said that it is the key to the whole problem of human life. We are not concerned here with the tremendous philosophical thesis that blind chance can produce out of chaos, without direction or purpose or intelligence, a state of affairs — that is human life on the earth — in which we find all three. Our question looks much simpler: can we expect to change ourselves simply by our own native wit and determination? In our own case, we do not need to shut out the rest of the world as philosophers must do in studying such questions as "Could life have arisen on the earth by blind chance?" We can at least draw upon the available knowledge of what can be done and how.

The question must, therefore, be more carefully framed. Can we change ourselves by our own native wit, plus what we can learn from others, plus our own determination? My personal belief, based on nearly fifty years' experience, is that we need 'something' that does not reduce to any of the three elements I have discussed so far: that is, learning, struggle and sacrifice. This 'something' resembles what is called in chemistry a **catalyst,** which acts in a marvellous way to make an almost impossible process go quickly and easily. For example, everyone has heard of polythene and we all use it in some form every day. When it was first made thirty years ago, huge steel towers capable of withstanding enormous pressures had to be used to produce it, and it was so expensive that in the war it could only be used for the most special purposes. Then the chemists discovered suitable catalysts and now polythene is made quickly, easily and cheaply in vast quantities. The catalyst does not 'produce' polythene but it 'helps' the reaction that does produce it.

My own belief is that the transformation of man is by nature such a slow and difficult process that scarcely one person in a hundred million could accomplish it in a lifetime, but that help is available which makes it possible for quite ordinary people to achieve it.

Help is like knowledge inasmuch as it has to enter our present moment from outside or beyond. It is unlike knowledge inasmuch as it does not enter through the mind. It is different in yet another way, namely, that it does not come from the same 'time' and 'space' as our minds and bodies live in. This is why it cannot be 'taken' or 'bought' as knowledge can be gained by learning, and strength by struggle and freedom by sacrifice.

All this may seem very mysterious, but let us consider a simple case of help. Once Gurdjieff showed me an exercise which required that one should remember to say 'I am' every hour at the exact moment, neither a minute early nor a minute late. I struggled desperately to do this exercise and failed completely. At most, I remembered five or six times out of sixteen waking hours. I tried all kinds of devices for reminding myself, but they only worked for a short time and none of them enabled me to carry out the exercise completely. Then one day Gurdjieff called me into his room and said: "You cannot make the exercise. I will lend you some of my **Hanbledzoin.**" For the next three days without any effort, I remembered almost to the second. I had such confidence that I put the exercise right out of my mind in the intervening time and yet I never forgot.

He did not explain anything, nor show me by his example how it could be done. He did not even encourage me. And yet I knew that 'something' had entered me and that as long as it lasted I would be able to do what was impossible.

Gurdjieff explained this kind of help to me in August 1923 when I was at the Prieuré in Fontainebleau. I can reproduce the conversation almost exactly, because I wrote it to my wife the same day and she preserved the letter. I had just such a demonstration of Gurdjieff's ability to help one to accomplish the impossible, when he said to me: "A man who wishes to change must have the necessary energy. Say he needs 100 units, but with all his efforts he can only collect 10. He is helpless. Suppose he meets a man who has more energy than he needs for himself. That man can lend him 90. Then he will do what he wants. Afterwards he must repay. Now you cannot do anything by yourself, so I must help you. There is a special substance — let us call it "higher emotional energy" that you need. You do not know where to get this substance, but I know. Later you will know too and then you will understand this work. Those who can give this substance to others who need it belong to a special section of the highest caste of humanity." I said to him: "How can I get the help I need?" He replied — we were talking in Turkish — "When you say **Amār** (Mercy!) with all your being. Only then can you be helped."

This conversation may give the impression that the helper himself produces, or even creates, the substance. It is not so. He is really more like a channel of transmission. His secret and his achievement are that **he has found the way to connect himself to a source which is outside of his own Present Moment.** He can transmit because the person helped enters into his present moment and can benefit from what he himself receives.

Help by the transmission of substances can be of many kinds and many degrees. The example I have just given is somewhere in the middle of the spectrum. There are quite simple people whose very presence 'does you good'. We say that they 'radiate goodness', or confidence or faith. We do not see the significance of such statements, chiefly because we constantly fail to notice the obvious. Not all people have the same quality of being. When we feel better because we have spent an hour with a certain person, it is because that person 'has something' and has it in the most literal sense. He is connected to an invisible source and because he probably does not know it, and certainly does not talk about it, we do not recognize how strange and how important it is.

In the Introduction, I wrote about what the Hindus call **Darshan** and the Sufis **Sohbat.** This is entering the presence of a holy man in order to benefit from his power to help. This power can be very intense, but it does not often produce a permanent change. Nevertheless, all who have felt it can confirm that it is due to a tangible "something" that can almost be felt in the air. Everyone I know who visited the Shivapuri Baba has agreed with me that one could feel it when one entered his compound even before turning the corner of the path at the end of which the Baba could be seen. I have met several men and one woman who had this power in different degrees.

Another form of it is in what the Chaldeans called **Hvareno,*** or the power associated with kingship. The Egyptians ascribed this power pre-eminently to the Pharaohs, on whom the entire welfare of their people was believed to depend. For three thousand years, it was believed that true kings had the power to cure certain sicknesses. The 'King's Evil' was still believed in up to the time of the Stuart Kings. There is probably a substantial foundation for such beliefs.

Now we must try to get a clearer picture of what this substance — or these substances — are. I think that there is not one substance which always acts to promote every kind of transformation, but many specific substances after the style of catalysts in chemistry. Chemical catalysts are mostly highly specific, each one produces changes of a definite kind and it is noteworthy that the nearer these catalysts approach the level of living things, the more specific they become. Enzymes such as yeast are very definite in their action. Hormones are almost certainly living complexes when they are in action. They have many characteristics that fit the description that I have given of 'help-substances' and are used for that very purpose by physicians today. I think it is reasonable to suppose that there are even more potent catalytic substances that are more like

---

*cf. *The Herald of Coming Good*, G. I. Gurdjieff, p. 12 and *The Dawn and Twilight of Zoroastrianism*, R. C. Zaehner, pp. 150-153.

patterns of energy than chemical compounds. The remarkable phenomenon of homeopathic medicine provides direct evidence that 'something' very potent indeed remains when the natural product is almost entirely removed by dilution. Homeopaths talk of a 'potency' of a thousand which means that not a single molecule of the original substance is likely to be present in the dose taken. There is also some reason — not so clear or convincing I am afraid — for supposing that 'radiations', quite different from light or other electro-magnetic vibrations, can cure or otherwise help people at a distance. I would classify these as physical agents in spite of the fact that they cannot be detected by physical means at present available.

There are other kinds of help in which the action does not seem to be through the organism, but works directly in the psyche. I believe that this is also some kind of substance or energy and it has different qualities and actions. These "psychic energies" can be transmitted from one person to another and when they are blended in the consciousness of the transmitter they are probably the same as the **Hanbledzoin** referred to in Gurdjieff's talk with me.

Finally, there are higher or 'spiritual' helps. This leads us into the domain of the supernatural. If we believe in miracles, we should probably be right to ascribe them to these higher or spiritual energies.

With these definitions of what I mean by 'help' and 'help' substances I shall now try to explain how I understand the role of help in the transformation of man.

We are trying to achieve an harmonious state of being in which we are free to fulfil the purpose of our existence. This means, first of all, bringing order into the chaotic state of our inner life — I hope that the reader will agree that our inner life is very little under our control and is very far from a state of stable harmony.

If disorder can produce order by its own activity — which is much to be doubted — it certainly does so far too slowly to be of much use to us in our own lifetimes. If so, then help is a crucial factor and we must find the way to obtain it.

The kind of help we are looking for is one that will enable us to do, with reasonable hope of success during the limited time we have between birth and death, what in theory at least we could do without help. I cannot make any 'rules' about help, because its nature is to be spontaneous and unconstrained. We cannot command it to come to us, nor even 'earn' it. This is why it is said that true help has always a gratuitous character. There is, in religion, a special sin called simony which is committed by those who are able to help others and look for a material reward. The principle here is that the 'help-substance' cannot be the property of anyone. Those who can be sources of help transmit it, even when the substances they transmit are partly produced by their own efforts.

I shall therefore summarize some of the situations in which I have had a personal experience of help.

1. The presence of people who have completed their transformation or are on the way to it. These are commonly called "holy men". I have described some ways in which they help.

2. Visiting places in which intensive transformation has occurred. These are "holy places" or sanctuaries. I would include visits to the tombs of saints, because in

my personal experience such visits can produce extraordinary results.

3. The help given by a teacher to his pupils. This presupposes a teacher who has made a contact with a Source of help. This kind of help can be very specific, because the teacher can choose the right time and place to give it. The teacher-pupil relationship facilitates the transmission.

4. Special rituals or ceremonies in which the transmission is made. This is called initiation. Each kind of initiation brings the initiate into contact with a particular help-substance or possibly a combination of several. When initiation is authentic — and I am afraid this is rather seldom — the initiate receives a permanent link with the source of help and is taught how to draw upon it when necessary.

I must emphasize my conviction that initiation is a specific and not a general contact. I have myself received several initiations and I have received help from all of them. But the help has been quite different in each case. Generally, one is required to keep the details and even the fact of initiation secret so I cannot describe them by name. To illustrate my point, one initiation had a startling, and, up to the present time, continuing effect on my health and energy. This initiation was offered to me on the grounds that I had important work to do and needed strength. At the time my health was failing, since then it has even improved. In another case, the initiation was described as a purifying action, and I can confirm that it has helped me to overcome a number of unpleasant defects in myself that I could not conquer by my own efforts. In yet another case, the initiation was for the purpose of communicating without external contact. This was some fifteen years ago and despite the fact that I have not had any external exchange during all this time, I can always renew the inner link with the source. The point is that these different helps did just what they were claimed to do, but nothing else.

I have compared this action to the selectivity of a radio receiver. There are various stations transmitting at different wavelengths. One can learn how to tune in to station A, in which case one will receive that programme and no other. Station B will give its own programme, but not that of station A.

The trouble is that people who group themselves round these sources of help tend always to claim too much. They verify in their own experiences that something really does happen and they suppose that all sorts of other things must be possible as well. There is in man a great tendency to 'wishful thinking'. With very slender evidence, a whole body of dogmatic claims is built up. The sad part of it is that when the unsound claims are disproved the entire action is discredited. Then, the fanatical adherents hold on to the action with even greater conviction and the disappointed become unduly critical and often hostile. In this way, many sources of help genuinely useful for man fail to fulfil their original promise.

5. I must now refer to spiritual or supernatural help. This is called **Grace** and its action is of two kinds: personal and communal. The former reaches the innermost nature of man and enables him to live a transformed life. The latter — called charismatic — gives people various powers — of healing, prophecy, interpretation. The charismatic help is well described by St. Paul in several epistles, particularly 1 Corinthians 12. I shall not dwell upon supernatural help,

because this is not a religious or devotional book. I can only state my personal conviction that supernatural, spiritual help is a reality and that it works throughout the truly religious life of man irrespective of any particular form of belief.

6. Spontaneous and unaccountable help. I must put this in a separate category for it is a strange phenomenon that is, above all, characterized by being noncausal. "The spirit bloweth where it listeth." All kinds of people in all kinds of situations find that moments come when doors seem to open by themselves, when the impossible becomes not merely possible but easy. One can call this Inspiration, but it does not cover all the varieties. Without this kind of help, I think human life would soon be overtaken by a progressive disintegration on every scale from private to planetary existence.

7. Finally, I come to the help that comes in moments of utter despair. This is different from spontaneous help because it is clearly connected with a visible and tangible situation. Gurdjieff explained it by saying "Nature hates vacuum. When you make empty, help will enter." There is, however, a strangely purposive quality about this kind of help. Nearly everyone I have asked — and there have been hundreds — confirms that they have unmistakably received help of this kind. It is referred to in innumerable proverbs and fables of all peoples and all times, so it must be a general heritage of mankind.

It is as if there were a great Universal Reservoir of help substances which ordinarily we cannot tap, but to which we have a secret channel. In moments of despair the channel opens and help substance flows in.

With that I shall end this chapter on the four sources: the reader can probably fill in many gaps for himself. Those interested in Systematics will find elsewhere in my writings* an explanation of why there should be four sources related in these particular ways.

---

*eg: *The Dramatic Universe,* Vol III p. 29 ff and 138 ff

" *Chess is really a comparatively simple activity, and it has been played by people of astonishing mental powers for several hundred years, and yet, out of the innumerable games that have been played, no game has ever been won except by the mistakes of one of the players.*

If this is true about chess, it is not surprising to find that it is also true about life, which is a very much more complicated game. The rules of life are not to be found neatly written down in books which one can buy for sixpence; they are very hard to discover and, strangely enough, no one ever attempts to discover them. "

THE CRISIS IN HUMAN AFFAIRS

Chapter Two

NECESSARY KNOWLEDGE

WE NEED TO KNOW ENOUGH about ourselves, about people in general and about the universe to be able to organize our lives sensibly and to achieve the degree of transformation that is possible for us. This knowledge need not be very complicated or complete: we need only know what is required for action. I am going to suggest ways of study for each of the different subjects to be known.

1. THE HUMAN BODY

My body is the home in which my mind or soul has to live from birth to death. It is the chief instrument by which I act on the world and achieve my purposes. Its state of health and efficiency — not just at this moment, but for the rest of my life — will influence everything that I think, feel, say and do.

All this is simply to say that my first duty is to take proper care of this unique instrument. For this, first of all, I must know it thoroughly well. I must know it as a living organism, and I must know also the peculiarities of this particular body.

Food

I must know what food is good for my body and what food is harmful. How much to eat and how often. What to drink and what to avoid. These requirements are different for different people and must be found out. Eating too much, or too little, can cause our bodies to deteriorate rapidly.

61

Breath

Most people usually breathe badly because they have never learned to breathe properly. We must remember that the sitting posture is unnatural for the human body and causes defective functioning — especially of the respiratory system. We need to correct this by learning how to breathe normally. Defective breathing shortens life.

Posture

Not only is the sitting posture unnatural for us but our way of life tends to produce habitual postures that interfere with blood circulation, strain the nervous system and have marked effects on our mental states. We must learn how to hold our bodies correctly in sitting, standing, walking and even in lying down.

Senses

Most people do not understand how to use their eyes, ears, sense of smell, taste and touch. They do not guess how much they lose by failing to train their sense perceptions.

Movements

All movements of the human body will consume energy. Clumsy and unnecessary movements not only harm the body's functioning, but they influence the state of the mind and feelings. We should learn about the natural rhythms of bodily movement and also the ways in which rhythmical movement can be controlled.

The Skin

The skin of man is one of the most critical areas of contact with his surrounding world. He takes in and gives out various energies and substances through his skin. We should know how to maintain the activity of the skin. People — especially women — do many foolish things to their skin. The human body differs from that of most animals in being provided with sweat-glands. Sweating is an important means of removing harmful substances from the body, but people do not understand this mechanism and many others that have been disorganized by the conditions of modern life.

Energies

We must not let ourselves forget that the human body developed its present construction during the Ice Age under far more severe conditions than we have today. Its entire functioning is geared to physical activity. When this is neglected, it is not only the condition of the muscles, but every system: nervous, digestive, respiratory, and especially the state of the blood that will deteriorate. Excessive athletic effort is scarcely less harmful than a sedentary life. The point is that one should study one's body and establish for oneself at suitable intervals — say every five years — how much exercise is right for maintaining good health.

In insisting on the importance of knowing one's body, I may seem to be advocating a kind of obsession with one's own state of health that is notoriously harmful to one's mental equilibrium. This risk will disappear if we remember to look upon the body as an instrument to be used. We are not concerned with its pains and aches, its desires and impulses; but with its good functioning. We must be able to gauge the demands we can safely make of it. Many people are afraid of hurting their bodies, of over-tiring themselves, of damaging some organ. This is the morbid attitude to be avoided. There is much to be said for the rough sports of boyhood. I myself have been thankful all my life that I had a passion for Rugby football and broke arms and ankles before I was twenty. I am also thankful for my time on the Western Front in 1917/8 when I learned that one could sleep in cold mud, or not sleep at all for forty-eight hours without harm.

To KNOW one's body, its powers and limitations, is very different from being compulsively interested in it or concerned about it.

Unfortunately, it is not easy to find teachers who can help us to know our bodies in the way I have described. We have to do it scientifically for ourselves — by observation and experiment.

2. THE MIND

We can look upon the mind as our 'inner' home, as the body may be called the 'outer' home. So far as our experience of ourselves and the world goes, we live 'in our minds'. I have put it in this way to emphasize the distinction between 'I' and 'my' mind which is as definite and easy to verify as the distinction between 'I' and my body.

I am not my mind

Before we go on to ask ourselves what the mind is, and how it works, we must satisfy ourselves that we know the answer to the question, "Am I my mind?" or put differently, "Is there anything in me that is not either mind or body?" For me personally, the answer admits of no doubt. Whenever I observe what is going on in my mind (it does not matter for the moment what we 'mean' by mind. We can call it the total content of the stream of experience partly noticed and partly unnoticed by 'me') I always find a non-mental element that I call 'I'. This leads me to say that 'I' am not 'my mind', nor any part of it. 'I' am not my thoughts, trivial or sublime; nor my feelings, my joys and sorrows; nor my sensations of pleasure and pain, not even the rare and wonderful insights which convince me that there is a higher Reality that I can hope to reach. 'I' am not even of the same kind as any of these. So I say that I have a direct certainty that 'I' am not my mind.

Our mind is our inner home

In some way, 'I' live in my mind. I do not seem to be there all the time, because I do not know where I am when I am asleep or in a coma. Even when 'I' am lost in day-dreams or wholly concentrated upon some manual task so that I am no longer aware of my mental processes, it seems right to say that I am no longer 'in my mind'. There certainly does seem to be some recognizable meaning in the phrase 'going out of one's mind'. So it is probably not far out to say that I live in my mind in much the same way as I live in my house. I am usually there and it is the centre of my life, but I am not always to be found 'at home'.

It seems also that there are regions of the mind that we seldom or never visit. There is the 'Bluebeard's Room' of the subconscious against which Freud and his followers warn us and yet tell us we must learn to live with. There are also mental experiences so unusual and wonderful that we remember them all our lives and may be drawn by this memory to find the way to them again.

The mind is like an old house containing secret chambers and store-rooms, and also built upon several storeys. We do not know it well enough and we miss much of the best of life by living mainly in the basement or, at best, the ground floor.

The mind has different functions

If you were asked 'What is your mind for?' you would answer, "It is for thinking". But our thinking is influenced by the state of the body — especially in so far as awareness of this state enters our mind. A violent toothache, alcoholic intoxication, a migrane will destroy for the time being our ability to think. Strong emotions will so colour our thoughts that they cease to be rational or even coherent. A fixed emotional prejudice will prevent us from accepting the clearest argument. Exciting sights or sounds will distract us from our thinking.

These are all going on 'in the mind'. The different activities can go on side by side without interfering, and they can also combine and reinforce one another. The simplest way of accounting for these observations is to say that there are different mechanisms for thinking, for emotional states and for experiencing sensastions of sight, sound, pain and so on. Gurdjieff calls these mechanisms 'centres' or 'brains' and distinguishes three principal ones: intellectual, emotional and instinctive-motor. I have called these 'mechanisms' and they should be studied as such. For more than forty years I have based my understanding of my own mental processes on this scheme and have found that it always works. So have thousands of others who have followed some branch of Gurdjieff's 'System'.

The study of the centres should be entirely practical, e.g.:

Instinctive — Motor Centre

Observe that your body has a 'mind of its own'. It

has above all its own skills that you cannot reproduce by thought or feeling. It has its own memory of places, actions, connectednesses. Its mind works far more rapidly than thought. We can observe this speed not only in moments of crisis, but in many situations where very rapid adjustments are required to execute a difficult bodily action. Many thousands of sensory impulses and muscular adaptations take place in the time that we can have a single thought. This is all part of 'knowing the body' that I outlined in the last section. It is useless to take it as 'interesting theory'; its value to us comes when we verify it and make it our own.

Emotional Centre

Our emotions have their own mind. Its main function is to concentrate the driving energy that enables us to act effectively. This energy is not blind and indiscriminating, but rather directed and purposeful. Our emotional centre gives an instantaneous direction to our activity. The direction may be different from or even opposite to that which our thinking mind would select and there may be a conflict between the two.

Another way of looking at the emotional centre is to take it as the seat of the mechanical, unreflective 'decisions' that govern most of our lives. We should see for ourselves that these decisions are seldom rational and yet they engage us and commit us to actions. When the emotional decision coincides with what we see intellectually to be reasonable and right for us, we can act with 'peace of mind' because there is not a conflict 'within the mind'. But we must also observe and verify for ourselves that the emotional decision has a force that cannot come from the most rational and clear thought. The emotional centre is the source of

67

our strength. If it is stable and coherent, our behaviour is strong and consistent.

Finally, we must learn to recognize that there are emotional 'insights'. These penetrate more rapidly and more deeply than thought into the complexity of a situation. They give us a special kind of 'knowledge' that can seldom be expressed adequately in words. This intuitive knowledge is very important for us because everything that comes from the emotional centre carries conviction. We want to believe it and are ready to ignore any intellectual objections that may arise in our minds. It is, therefore, important that we should understand its limitations and learn not to trust our 'intuitions' unless we can find a way to confirm them. We can do this by observing how often we find that our 'intuitive certainty' proves to be mistaken. We need intuitions: life would be colourless and too passive without them. The point here is that we should find out for ourselves just how our own emotional centre works and take what we find into account in learning to manage our lives.

Intellectual Centre

We do our thinking mainly by means of 'inner conversation', using ordinary language as if we were talking to ourselves. This kind of thinking is necessarily limited by the instruments it uses: by words. We cannot **think** 'in words' what cannot be **said** 'in words'. The intellectual centre is not by its nature dependent upon words. It can use any kind of image or symbol: but it cannot work without some form of **representation**. This is both its strength and its weakness. It is a strength because we can represent not only what is happening here and now, in this Present Moment, but also what

68

has happened or will happen or is happening elsewhere. This is a wonderful operation and it probably distinguishes man from animals. **By means of thought we can go outside our present moment,** not only in the dimensions of time and space, but also into the timeless dimensions of logic and form. The greater part of our characteristically human activity depends upon our ability to project our thoughts outside the present moment. No doubt animals have memory, but there is no sign that they can voluntarily construct out of their memories images of past events or expectations of future events. With them 'out of sight' is almost certainly 'out of mind'. With man, it is only relatively so.

We do not study our thought processes with sufficient objectivity. Here is a marvellous instrument to be used: we spend many years in training it, but very little time in learning how it works. There are various techniques that can be used to develop in the thinking centre the ability to think without either words or visual images.

The intellectual centre, like the others, has a variety of functions and can work on different levels. One combination must be studied and known: the associative mechanism, by which we produce coherent sequences of ideas and words. This mechanism was called by Gurdjieff **the formatory apparatus,** because it can produce coherent forms of thought and speech, but cannot formulate or express new and original notions. Because this apparatus is closely linked to the brain, it is constantly stimulated by every kind of impression received from outside and it reacts mainly by habitual sequences of words, spoken or unspoken.

We tend to mistake the work of this mechanism for true thought, partly because it is active all the time, and partly because it can produce appropriate responses to 'thought-questions'. This 'formatory thinking' is very deceptive. It is easily trained to say 'the right thing at the right time'. Nowadays, we have begun to suspect this sort of conditioned cleverness. It tends to produce 'yes-men' who say and do what is expected of them. It makes people who are almost defenceless against 'mass-media' propaganda. The enormous availability of the printed word tends to produce a constant automatic interaction between the visual impact of words and the associative mechanism of the formatory apparatus. Among other disadvantages, this makes it very hard to bring into action the more conscious and creative parts of the intellectual centre.

On account of its mechanical operation, the formatory apparatus has little or no capacity for initiative, and it is chiefly set in motion by impulses coming from the sexual, emotional and sensory-motor centres.

I have not attempted to give an exhaustive account of the centres and their work. The important thing is to study them for oneself. They are differently formed and developed in different people and each one of us needs to know his or her own peculiarities. Special exercises are needed to study the formatory apparatus properly.

Levels of Function

As I have dealt with this subject in several books and papers,* I shall give only a summary here. The basic ideas are derived from Gurdjieff, but they are so hard to disentangle in his presentation that we made a fresh

---

*e.g. *How we do things,* and *Creative Thinking* C.S.P.

start at the Institute for Comparative Study and after several years of experiment and observation produced a scheme that is, in my opinion, of the greatest value both for education and training in everyday life and also for those who are drawn towards transformation and the attainment of a higher level of being.

The first notion to grasp is that everything that happens in all material, living, mental or even spiritual processes involves the transformation of **energy.** This is obvious both in non-living and living bodies that can be studied by physical and biological scientists. It is, therefore, no great step to assume that the same is true for the processes that occur in our minds. Every thought, every sensation, every emotion is produced by energy exchanges, but the energies are different, or at least **in a different state,** from those that produce bodily movements or chemical changes.

There are twelve great orders or levels of energy: four in the material world, four in the world of living things and four in the spiritual world.* Only five of these directly concern the human mind and so I shall describe these five only, starting from the highest and most powerful. They are numbered E1, E2, etc. from the highest downwards.

E3: Creative Energy

This is a supra-conscious energy beyond the ordinary associative operations of the mind and yet it has a great importance for us, for, as its name implies, it is the source of all truly creative activity.

It does not work directly in or through the three centres and therefore we can know it only by its results.

*cf. *Energies,* C.S.P.

We cannot observe it in operation. That is why all truly creative work has the quality of **spontaneity and unexpectedness.** It comes, as we say, 'out of the blue'. The results may come in the form of new and really original moments of intellectual insight. We call them quite rightly 'flashes of genius'. It can also come in direct unspoken communication, whereby two people discover that they are united. It is experienced most directly in sexual union, when this is the true act of sacrifice described in Chapter 1. There is emotional creativity by which great decisions are taken. Instinctive-motor creativity is a necessary element in all creative work in art and science.

E4: Conscious Energy

This corresponds to the highest level of mental experience. Consciousness is an universal energy that is not confined within our own private, present moment. When our 'I' is in the conscious region of the mind, it is **able to stand apart** from the mind. It is very important to recognize and verify this statement, because it will enable you to test for yourself what 'consciousness' really means. It gives an added dimension to our mental experience, a dimension that is 'in depth' rather than in time and space.

Conscious energy makes it possible to criticize and judge ourselves and our mental processes by standing apart from them.

Conscious energy allows original constructive activity in all the centres and when it is present it can bring the three centres into a single field of experience. This does not always happen because it can also be concentrated in one place. When the centres work on the conscious level, we are aware of being free to think, to feel and to act as we decide and not as we are impelled by external influences and habits.

I must emphasize that I am using the word 'conscious' in a rather different way from what is usual.

E5: Sensitive Energy

We are 'aware' of what is going on by means of the sensitive energy. As we usually take 'aware of' to mean the same as 'conscious of', this definition needs some explanation. I use the word 'awareness' in a very wide sense to mean any kind of experience. We are aware of sights and sounds, of pain or discomfort, of feeling well or out of sorts. We are also aware of thoughts, mental associations, emotions, intuitions, insights, On the rare occasions when we are truly conscious, we are **aware of being conscious.** So I would say that all experience is awareness, but awareness can be on different levels. The highest is consciousness (since creativity is beyond consciousness) and the lowest is automatism (which we will come to next). The usual state of the mind is that of sensitivity, in which it is **aware of what is happening in the present moment in one of the centres** and unaware of what is going on in the others. The commonest state is that of being aware only of the activity of the formatory apparatus: we can recognize this as a kind of pointless inner conversation that we are holding with ourselves or nobody. This is interrupted when our attention is drawn to some sight, sound or other bodily sensation. This observation may help us to recognize the character of the sensitive energy: it produces a localized awareness and not a general consciousness of what is present. It can be compared to a torch that will light up what it is focussed on, but will not light up the room. Consciousness is like having a bright light in the middle of the room.

Another way of studying sensitive energy is to think of it as a kind of **sticky substance** that holds two surfaces in contact. When some part of one of our centres gets stuck in this way we call it 'being attentive' and the moment of sticking we call 'noticing'. By studying — as we can in a few days — what happens when we pass from a state of not-noticing to one of noticing, we can convince ourselves that a special 'something' is at work. This 'something' is what I call sensitive energy. For example, I am seated at my desk writing. I do not notice the colour of the writing pad although I have been looking at it for half-an-hour. Then something **makes** me notice it. I am aware of being connected with it in a way I was not a moment ago.

These fluctuations of sensitive energy are going on all the time and sometimes we notice with quite a shock that we are speaking and not attending to what we are saying, or reading without following the meaning of the words. Such observations help us to see how 'we' can be in a part of our mind without being aware of it.

E6: Automatic Energy

Our centres can function with no awareness of being connected with what is going on and yet the action can be quite well coordinated and effectual for its purpose. We usually walk in this way without noticing how we walk. Most of our instinctive processes go on without sensitivity. Some energy must be keeping them going: I call this 'automatic'.

Automatic functioning of our centres is the basic state of our waking and sleeping existence. Automatism without sensitivity is far more frequently our state than we ever realize, for the simple reason that **we do not notice the automatic functioning.**

The automatic energy is at the lowest limit of the mind: below this the functions are physiological rather than mental. It is at the minimum degree of awareness to qualify as a 'mental' energy and yet it is necessary for the normal functioning of the mind. The sensitive energy is in a constant state of flux — we are familiar with this in the form of 'mind-wandering' — and our actions would lose all their coherence if there were not a mental mechanism that could 'work without attention'.

E7: Vegetative Energy

Our mental activity is supported all the time by a physiological activity, especially of course that of the nervous system and the chemical life of the blood. Our organism has its own regulative mechanism that helps and, if necessary, restores the balance of its extremely complex functions. We are vaguely aware of the abnormal functioning of this regulator even when it does not produce painful or otherwise noticeable symptoms. We are also aware of what it is like to feel in a state of active, normal health. It seems, therefore, right to include the vegetative energy of the organism among those that are connected with mind.

Probably all the activity in the region between the automatic and vegetative energies belongs to the "subconscious" mind. It certainly influences that part of the mind that we usually call 'conscious'.

It is, in my opinion, extremely useful for all who are interested in learning or teaching, in improving their mental powers, or in transforming to higher levels, to familiarize themselves with the notion of these five energies and five corresponding levels of function. This can be done partly by observation and experiment and partly by studying various activities of man, from works of genius in art or science to the most ordinary routine of everyday life, and setting down the combinations of energies and functions needed to achieve them. This exercise is revealing and rewarding. It is worth doing conscientiously, because one will find that very much in human life will become clear to us in doing so.

We have found that the entire range of scientific, human and spiritual phenomena that can be observed or described can be described and even explained in terms of twelve energy levels, ranging from heat, the lowest and least organized form of energy, to a supposed supreme energy that governs the entire process of the Universe. There are various kinds or qualities within each level. For example, there are sensation-energy, feeling-energy, thought-energy, all on the level of the sensitive energy E5. Combinations and blends of different energies can produce special results. It is also probable that the higher energies can organize themselves in stable form. I am convinced that there are 'thought-forms' that can be produced by certain mental exercises and that these can influence and organize the coarser energies. The phrase 'mind over matter' certainly stands for something that does happen and is important.

The principle is a simple one: each higher energy has the power of organizing the lower ones. Sensitivity can direct the work of our automatism. When I say 'I will sit down and write', it is the sensitive energy that organizes the required series of movements. Consciousness can organize sensitivity, as when we make the decision to struggle with some defect or to concentrate our attention upon a particular theme. The decision is made by our will, but it is executed by the conscious energy, which has power over our thoughts and feelings. This example shows, however, that there is a limit set by the quantity of conscious energy available at a given moment. We can easily verify this by observing how we can sustain an active, critical interest in a book we are reading or a theme on which we are meditating for a certain time and then suddenly our attention extinguishes like a lamp that has run out of oil. What was easy a minute ago, has become impossible. We rest for a few minutes, or better still do some physical exercise, and we find our 'fuel is replenished'. We can verify that the fuel in question is not that which enables us to read or to think (because these can continue without critical attention), but a consciousness that is **behind** the reading or thinking. We can suppose that the still higher and more powerful creative energy can **organize consciousness.** This makes sense of the observation so often reported by artists and thinkers that in their moments of inspiration they **find** or discover rather than **construct** the intuitive leap ahead that they are making. In certain circumstances this creative energy can act on several people simultaneously, and this accounts for the frequency with which important discoveries are made independently by people who have no knowledge of one another's work.

3. MIND AND SOUL

The most plausible objection to the belief that man has a soul is that we cannot find anything like it when we look into our minds and their working. Nor can we see that any part of our behaviour is attributable to a supposedly non-material spiritual principle separate from the mind.

Now, the 'question of the soul' is obviously important. Most people nowadays believe that it has been disposed of for good by the science of psychology (which means literally the 'science of the soul', but prides itself on dispensing with the hypothesis) and that even the mind is only an activity of the brain. As this chapter is about 'knowledge', we must see if there is any way of reconciling the mechanistic or materialistic view of man, with the belief that there is in him 'something' which is not just matter in motion. We should make the attempt if only because it is hard to believe that our 'I' — that in us which experiences joy and suffering, which wants to know and understand what life is all about — is nothing at all but a chemical or electrical phenomenon, or some other mechanical product.

It is not enough to say 'I cannot and will not abandon the belief that I have a soul'. There was a time when men said that they could not and would not abandon the belief that the earth is the centre of the Universe. Some still believe that man is the summit of creation and that the entire existing Universe was created for the benefit of man. I have met intelligent Moslems who had no doubt about it, nor did they doubt that everything that happens in the world is directly regulated by God, without the intervention of natural laws. How are we to be sure that even if the non-existence of the soul has not yet been decisively established, it will be demonstrated before long by some decisive scientific experiment? The reader unfamiliar with early Buddhist scriptures may be interested to know that the Buddha is claimed to have demonstrated — more than 2,500 years ago, by simple scientific tests — that man has no soul. This is the origin of the so-called **Avatta** or no-soul doctrine in Buddhist psychology.

I myself was entirely bewildered by this question until I heard Gurdjieff's simple explanation: "Man has not a soul unless and until it is formed in him. He has the possibility of a soul and he has the materials out of which a soul can be made, but unless he makes it these materials have no permanent structure and after the death of the body they will be dispersed and return to the place or state from which they came." I found this theory rather convincing and it agreed with my own personal conviction that the "unconditional immortality of the soul" which I had been taught at school could not be true. It leads to the doctrine, which always seemed monstrous to me, of eternal salvation or damnation for all. Quite apart from what psychologists might say, two things seemed certain to me. First, that I could find nothing in myself that was permanent and independent of the physical body. Second, that 'I' was not my body or my mind and that this 'I' had a potential for becoming something more than a precarious tenant of a perishable home whether I call this home body or mind or both.

For a long time, I was satisfied with the comparison of the soul-stuff to a 'crucible of metallic powders' with no permanent composition or shape, but which could be fused by heat, melted and converted into an alloy in the form of a nugget of stable composition and properties. I accepted that the 'heat' required to melt the powders was produced by the 'struggle of yes and no'.*

Twenty or thirty years passed during which I made

---

*This simile appears in Ouspensky's *In Search of the Miraculous*, on p. 43. It is attributed to Gurdjieff.

sincere efforts to keep this struggle going — sometimes very intensely, sometimes distracted by a very active outer life — but the fusion did not take place and I was as volatile and unstable at fifty as I had been at twenty. I began to ask myself if I had been barking up the wrong tree. Then various things began to happen and I found out for myself that not only heat but a 'flux' was needed. (The flux corresponds to the help about which I wrote in the last section of Chapter 1.) I also realized that struggle alone is an almost impossible way of generating the heat required and that by sacrifice one could quite change the process. Out of my experience during the last twenty years (i.e. since I was fifty) I have become convinced that soul-formation is possible and not really so terrifyingly difficult as it had seemed. I became sure that I had a soul when I discovered that it had been made out of a part of my mind and that it is, in fact, capable of existing apart from my physical body and that it is able to control and organize the energies of the body and the mind. I am convinced that the 'soul' is made of the same energies as the 'mind' by a process of organization and consolidation. **The soul is a mind made stable and independent of the body.** This last point is the important one. The materials out of which the soul is made (the 'soul-stuff' seems the best name for them) are at first dependent upon the support of the body: just as the metallic powders in Gurdjieff's example will not hold together without the support of the crucible. When the soul-stuff is organized and stabilized it is like the nugget that can be taken out of the crucible. Often the crucible has to be broken to get the nugget out and in a similar way man's physical body usually has to die to set the soul free.

80

The reader will not have failed to notice that my own conviction has evolved from emotional acceptance, to intellectual assent first and conviction afterwards, and from this to the certainty of direct experience. He may ask whether I suggest that 'knowledge of the soul' is to be gained only by fifty years of experimentation by trial and error.

This is such an important question that I must answer it as well as I can. It is, I believe, possible to convince oneself that the theory of the soul as something that is not born complete and immortal, but gradually formed during life, is plausible. It accounts well for the facts of our experience and accords with the experience of those who have acquired their soul. It contradicts the usual interpretation of Christian dogma — an interpretation that is far more Greek than Christian — according to which the soul enters man's body completely formed and leaves it as it came, except for the accumulated consequences of the life that has just ended, and that it will continue to exist in the same way for ever and ever. I think this is a mistaken interpretation that comes from confusing the 'I' or the Will or the Spirit of Man with the vehicle or vessel or body of the soul. The remarkable parable of the wedding garment (Matt. 22) and many of the sayings of Jesus recorded in the Gospels are wholly consistent with the belief that the soul may be 'gained or lost' ("What shall it profit a man if he gain the whole world and lose his own soul?"). This book is not the place for an exhaustive discussion of such a delicate question as the 'theology of the soul', so I shall pass on to the second stage.

Can one make any experiments or observations that tend to confirm the theory of soul-transformation? I shall return to this question several times in later chapters; but, meanwhile, I will make a suggestion. If you have agreed that your 'I' is not your mind nor any part of it, but something (or someone) who lives in the mind without being fixed in any one place, then you can go further and ask yourself how it is that your mind will sometimes **obey** your 'I' and at other times not. I said that this is connected with the presence of **conscious energy.** Now we can suppose that the conscious energy does this by providing the 'I' with a lever to act on the sensitive energies of thought and feeling. There is an affinity between the 'I' or Will and the conscious energy which enables them to unite and act upon other energies. I would call this a 'temporary soul'. Every time this union is made, it leaves some 'organised conscious energy' behind. In this way the soul gradually forms.

The point is that we can know what it **feels** like to have a soul even before we have acquired a 'real' one. It feels like **having a master within oneself that one's mind and body will obey.** With this goes a feeling of inner freedom and detachment from external things and also from mind and body.

The strength and coherence of the 'coating' of conscious energy surrounding the 'I' can vary enormously. It may be no more than enough to produce a state of observation without power to act. Everyone knows the state in which they 'see and hear' themselves acting foolishly or violently, quite contrary to the wish of their 'I' which is no more than a helpless onlooker.

At the other extreme, the concentration of conscious energy may be so great and it may be so well fused together by blending with sensitivity, that one finds that one is complete master of oneself. I remember when this first happened to me in 1949, when I was working closely with Gurdjieff. After a night of struggle and sacrifice, I found 'myself' completely free from 'myself' able to be and do whatever I chose. I could be astonished, love, fear, control my mind, and what is more, I knew that this was because something was present in me that had all the characteristics of the 'soul' I was in search of.

I say, therefore, that we can do a great deal to verify the 'soul-theory' and also to learn about the process of soul-formation; which is, after all an essential part of that transformation which is the main theme of this book.

4. THE UNIVERSAL LAWS

Although self-knowledge must come first, we need also to know how the world — and we as part of the world — do work and could work. I am not referring to scientific knowledge: which does not really tell us **how** things happen but rather **what** things happen. Science is concerned with discovering what things happen in a regular and predictable way, so that the knowledge can be used to make human activity more successful and also to open the way to further discoveries. For example, science knows an enormous amount about **what** 'electricity' does, but almost nothing about **how** it does it. Usually, this does not matter, because scientists and technologists are interested in results, and results are simply 'what happens when'.

When we enter the field of mental processes, an unpredictable element is involved: this is the fluctuation of consciousness that is spontaneous and uncontrollable — as we can easily verify beyond all doubt. Consequently, we can never predict what will happen at a given moment in a given mind. (I am speaking in the singular because there can be a statistically predictable **average** behaviour and this is what experimental psychology is mainly concerned with.) We have to invoke some principle other than cause and effect or maximum probability. We can no longer verify by repetition, because conscious actions do not repeat. This should not be surprising, if I am right in concluding that the 'higher' energies of consciousness, creativity and love are universal and can never be isolated and 'put in a test tube'. They can act on 'us', but 'we' cannot act on them. Any attempt to study them 'scientifically' would be like a guinea pig turning round to make experiments on the psychologist who has put him in the cage.

It does not follow that we have no way of understanding at least the broad principles of 'how' things work. There are universal laws that can be studied and applied to the solution of practical problems. These laws have been known and studied in the past under various forms and designations. I have taken the general term **Systematics** to stand for the study of the laws which govern the way in which the world works. These laws also govern **what** the world does, but indirectly, so that science in fact takes them into account without realizing it. So do successful practical men. I shall only describe here the three laws which seem to me to be the most important for understanding the hidden processes of our transformation.

1. The Law of Dynamism

This is also called the Law of Threefoldness or the Law of the Triad. It says, in effect, that cause and effect, or action and reaction, do not explain **how** things happen in the way they do. For this we must take the **Third Force** into account. This third force is genuinely mysterious because we cannot detect it in the way that we can detect and measure action and reaction. This does not mean that it is 'unscientific'. On the contrary, in every branch of science a mysterious third force keeps turning up. For example, in electricity we are used to the idea that like charges repel and unlike charges attract. Now, atoms are made of particles with positive charges (protons) and negative charges (electrons) and we should expect them either to fly apart or cancel out, according to whether they are like or unlike. It has been necessary to suppose that there is a third kind of force (exchange force or binding or meson energy) which acts in such a way as to 'reconcile' the contradiction of positive and negative. No one pretends to know what this is or **how** it works, but they are satisfied **that** it works. Modern physics is full of instances of remarkable results obtained by observing **what** happens while admitting to total ignorance of **how** it happens or even of what it happens **to.** Yet if one looks at all the marvellous achievements of modern physics — including astrophysics, which has taught us incredible things about the physical universe — we can always see that three independent factors are involved. I have called these factors the Affirming, Receptive and Reconciling Impulses. The Law of Dynamism says that the **how** of every kind of event depends upon the way these three impulses are combined. I shall not go further into this as it is easier to understand when we come across actual examples that we can test for ourselves.

2. The Law of Constructive Activity

This is also called the Law of the Tetrad. It tells us

how processes are kept going in such a way as to build up a state of order or coherence. We find that there are various factors that give the process its **direction** and others that provide it with the **means.** We call them motivational and instrumental **sources** of the activity. There is always some kind of Ideal or goal and there is a starting point or ground state. The line joining these is the direction of the process. There is also some kind of inner mechanism and some kind of outer driving force that can be compared to an engine and the fuel it runs on. These 'instrumental' terms can be extremely varied. In the working of our minds they may take the form of thought (the inner mechanism) and emotion (the driving energy).

The point is that without some appropriate construction and mutual adjustment of the four factors the process either flies to pieces or comes to a stop. I can illustrate it by taking the process of transformation described in Chapter One. There are four sources from which influences flow in to keep the process moving. Two of these give the direction: one is knowledge of our present situation and its potentialities and the other is the source of help which is also the Ideal or goal towards which we want to go. We have various means at our disposal: they are struggle and sacrifice and combinations in which both are involved. These four must stand in the relationship of Direction and Means. The means must not become ends: we must not struggle for struggling's sake, nor must we simply abandon what is precious to us as if throwing things away were an end in itself. Similarly, we must realize that knowledge by itself will not change us: it will only tell us that transformation is possible and in what direction it must go.

In planning any enterprise the four sources — or terms of the tetrad — should be looked for and defined. One should satisfy oneself that there will be an effective flow from each of the four and that they will be properly adjusted to one another.

3. The Law of Hazard

Every one knows from experience of large and small undertakings that all without exception are hazardous. Large ones can go wrong because of the multitude of unpredictable factors. Small ones may be carried along in the stream of larger ones: but they are subject to hazards outside their control: **forces majeures as we call** them. If in our experience we find hazard is always present, we should expect it to be universal outside our experience also. In other words, we should be ready to accept that there must be a Law of Hazard that enters into everything. If we look at life objectively, we see that hazard makes it interesting, exciting and worthwhile. If everything were governed by a strict law of cause and effect and one could always predict the outcome of an action, we might as well be a lot of mechanical toys wound up to walk and talk with no say in what we should or should not do. I took the title *Dramatic Universe* for my main work in order to emphasize that the Universe is interesting just because it is hazardous and therefore on every scale open to the drama of success and failure.

The Law of Hazard tells us that any process directed towards a definite aim is bound to be deflected by the reactions it produces and if these deflections are not compensated, the process will either come to a stop or change direction so completely as to 'become its own opposite'. It also tells us how the compensation can be achieved. This is basically by **the cooperation of pro-**

cesses of independent origin. Sometimes the two processes appear to be opposed or even in conflict and yet it is only by their mutual impact that they are kept going in a definite direction.

A familiar example is that of 'growing up'. From the moment of conception the new human being is dependent upon its parents. Without them it cannot be born, nor can it continue to live and develop after birth without parents, or failing them, foster-parents. The action of the parents is directed towards the development of a mature human being and yet the very dependence which the process requires will produce a 'mother's darling', or immature adult, unless it is compensated by the drive to independence coming from the contact the boy or girl develops with society. There is a conflict between the 'home' and the 'world' and yet it is out of the two opposing processes that right maturing is possible.

You must notice here that the **timing** is critical. The **impact** of the world must not come too soon or too late and it must not be too weak or too strong. The rightly timed impact is what Gurdjieff called a 'shock' and he formulated the Law of Hazard in terms of a musical octave which goes by tones and semi-tones from **do** to **do**. The semi-tones at mi-fa and si-do correspond to the points at which other processes must make their impact. Gurdjieff went so far as to call this the 'first primordial cosmic law'; and, although he did not use the expression Law of Hazard, the description he himself gives* means nothing else but this. In fact, his account is so obscure and indirect that I had virtually to rediscover the law for myself before I began to understand it.

---

*In *All and Everything*, Chapter 39

I am sure that it is very important for all of us to grasp and as far as we can to verify this Law of Hazard. It helps us to understand why so many well-intentioned activities for the good of mankind come to grief and even become their own opposite. Hitler undoubtedly started with the best intention of raising the morale of the German people and giving them a new sense of purpose and we all know how he ended. The reason is not so obvious. It is probably due to the fact that the world apathy of the seven fateful years 1932-9, prevented any strong counter-process from developing.

There is far, far more to be said about the Law of Hazard, but I want to avoid 'theorizing' as far as possible. The four examples of knowledge I have taken — body, mind, soul and universal laws — do not contain all that we need to know. I have chosen them because they are neglected in our education and because they give material that the intelligent reader can follow up and verify for himself. Perhaps I may finish this chapter by distinguishing between knowledge that is useful for acting upon the world about us and knowledge that is useful for acting upon ourselves. There is plenty and to spare of the first kind of knowledge: but it is not easy to find the second. Knowledge of the second kind is primarily for the purpose of transformation. But even for those who do not feel urged to embark on the difficult and hazardous undertaking of acquiring a soul, it is still useful to learn about man and how the working of his body and mind can be improved.

89

" Throughout all the different disciplines of school education runs one common thread: neglect of concrete meanings and reliance solely upon the ability to juggle with words. This is encouraged very strongly by the evaluation of the results of effort through oral and written examinations which no one attempts to relate to any inner understanding. One tragical effect of the whole process is the appearance throughout the world of millions of people completely defenceless against verbal suggestion. "

WHAT ARE WE LIVING FOR?

Chapter Three

COMMUNICATION

W E LIVE NORMAL HUMAN LIVES by sharing experience with others. The more we can share, the richer and fuller is our experience. Transformation towards a greater perfection will mean also more perfect sharing. The mark of the perfected man is his ability to share in the joys and sufferings, the foolishness and the wisdom of all mankind. We can take it then, that the ability to share — which means to communicate — develops as an integral part of the process of transformation. In this chapter, I shall trace some of the stages through which the power of communication can develop in us.

1. LISTENING

Observe and note how much and how well we listen to what other people are saying. Is our listening for the sake of communication or for criticism and self-assertion? Do we really try to understand: not only what is being said, but the intention of the speaker?

We should exercise ourselves regularly in the art of listening. We can make a special exercise of listening to people who do not hold our attention, saying things that do not interest us.

Listening leads us to the first requirement of communication: that is **receptivity.** We should learn to distinguish between passive receptivity, which is close to suggestibility and the indiscriminate acceptance of all that we hear; and dynamic receptivity which enables us to 'take in' what is said to us and relate it to what we already know and understand about the subject. Dynamic receptivity requires a positive act of will. We must learn to recognize this act and to make it whenever we wish to listen dynamically.

We can extend the notion of dynamic listening to all situations in which we set ourselves to grasp the **intention** of what is being conveyed to us. It applies to reading as much as to hearing. Few people know how to read in a state of dynamic receptivity. This is very different from either the passive uncritical swallowing of what the author says or the aggressive critical attitude that reads only to refute.

As our concern is with our possible transformation, we must be prepared to train ourselves from the start to put ourselves, whenever necessary, in the state of dynamic receptivity. This ability is always useful: it increases our capacity for profiting by opportunities that we might otherwise fail to notice. In transformation, it is more than useful: if we do not learn to listen and to notice what is being conveyed to us, we shall sooner or later come up against an obstacle which may make further progress impossible. This will occur when it becomes necessary for us to reach out and recognize what some wiser person wishes to convey, but cannot do so because we lack the experience or the sensitivity to understand.

Listening, in its widest sense, includes all kinds of dynamic perception. We must train ourselves to see better. Every specialist notices things connected with his own speciality that an untrained person would miss. A trained eye is no less necessary for communication than a trained ear. We must learn to notice the facial expressions, gestures, postures of people with whom we are conversing.

Exercises for developing the ability to make fuller use of our senses and their perceptions have a value beyond communication, and they have the advantage that they give tangible results that anyone can verify. They are, therefore, useful for beginners who have little experience on which to rely. They are not really elementary, for they can be deepened far beyond ordinary perception. There is an 'inner listening' that takes in usually unnoticed vibrations of sound and opens into a form of communication that is beyond the power of speech.

Some people are more sensitive than others to subtleties of sound and movement, but they tend to notice only what they themselves happen to feel and miss what is being conveyed in these subtleties. Those who are naturally insensitive find it hard to believe that they cannot take in what they are hearing and seeing. In both cases, exercise is needed. The ability to listen is very seldom innate in a person. Most of us need to work hard and persistently in order to achieve a dynamic contact with what we see and hear.

The appreciation of music and the fine arts is certainly a means of improving our perceptions. The artist must communicate or his work perishes. He is interested in evoking a dynamic response. It might seem, therefore, that the requirement we are looking for can be found in the arts. This is only partly true. It is possible to acquire an uncanny power of appreciating art and music and of interpreting the intentions of the artist, and yet to remain insensitive and unresponsive to people in the flesh. An artist may have a very great potential for transformation, but he may lose it if he cannot come to grips with personal communication.

In short, we all need to exercise ourselves constantly in the art of listening and seeing.

2. LANGUAGE

The urge to share experience is clearly present in the young child before he can articulate his first word; but he learns to speak about objects and actions, not about his own feelings and states. This initiates a divorce between what we **want** to say and what we **can** say that haunts us all our lives.

So long as we are satisfied with communications about things that we can see and touch and actions that we can demonstrate, our language can be a very effective instrument. When we want to talk about intangible things, we can only hope that our hearer understands the words we use with the same meaning as they have for us.

Unfortunately, many words and phrases that refer to our private experiences are very hard to verify. Others are used with complete disregard for their possible meaning. Among such words are several that refer to experiences and processes that are vitally important for our transformation. We must be able to communicate our inner problems and very often we find that no word will express what we need to say. We need advice and help in understanding ourselves and we need precise instructions about what we should do in the face of our inner problems.

When we face the problem of language, it might seem that we would need hundreds of words to express the seething complexity of our private experience.

When we look at it more closely, we find that quite a small number of words needs to be understood and their intended meaning shared in order to communicate successfully about 'inner world problems'. Everyone should make his own list of essential words and set about clarifying their meaning to himself. The following list is given to suggest how a start can be made, but I want to emphasize that the value of the exercise consists in examining one's own problems and trying to put them into words which another person would be sure to understand as we intend them. The twenty-one words I have chosen fall into three groups connected with who we are, with what we experience and with the way our inner world works. I shall call them 'who' words, 'what' words and 'how' words. These three groups may not suit everyone and I would certainly not expect everyone to construct the same list.

Key Words of the Inner Life of Man

'Who' Words	'What' Words	'How' Words
'I'	Sensation	Memory
Self	Feeling	Conscience
Individuality	Thought	Sincerity
Being	Consciousness	Attention
Will	Hope	Decision
Mind	Love	Presence
Soul	Faith	Understanding

To these twenty-one typical inner-life words, I would add the unclassifiable word **Freedom,** the key of all keys and the hardest word of all to understand. We use all these words liberally enough, but seldom stop to enquire what we really intend them to convey. It is hardly surprising that we have so little success in our inner life communications. We need to be sure that we really do wish and intend to communicate and not merely to 'talk about ourselves', which is a very different matter. It is not our likes and dislikes, our theories and views about the world, our adventures and experiences that matter, but who and what we really are and how we are to set about improving the situation.

All human beings are constructed on the same basic pattern, not only in their physical body but also in the mechanism of their inner life. We need to know this inner mechanism in order to communicate intelligently and usefully. Unfortunately we cannot dissect our minds and souls and see how the various parts are put together, nor can we demonstrate their working and describe or define the things that happen. We are forced to rely upon what we ourselves discover and out of this we must build up a language that we can share with others.

Two methods are available: one is self-observation and self-questioning and the other is mutual questioning and the sharing of experience with others. The two must be combined in order to bring the meanings of words into clear focus for ourselves and be able to share them with others.

The work of clarification is a real discipline. We must, at all costs, avoid morbid introspection or excessive interest in ourselves. Our interest must be directed to understanding the content of our experience in the same detached way as a chemist would examine a complex chemical compound. When we discuss the elements of the inner life with others, we should avoid what Gurdjieff condemned as 'wiseacring'; that is, inventing ideas that we cannot verify.

Both of these mistakes can be avoided by organized self-study. Various exercises for this will come up in later chapters. The creation of a common language comes best as a by-product of self-study and the exchange of experience. Nevertheless, some fixation of meaning is required and I shall suggest ways of looking at the words I have selected for my own list.

'I'

Anything that we can observe or even think about is 'not-I'. I am that which (or he who) observes and thinks and decides, and never the instruments by which observations and thoughts and decisions are made. We get into difficulties if we ask any more questions such as: "Am 'I' always the same?", "Am I one I or many I's?", "Do I exist or is the I-feeling merely a state of my mind or body?". Because we cannot answer such questions from direct observations, we have no means of verifying who or what "I am".

Self

When I speak of 'myself' to what do I refer? According to one teaching, we have not one but several 'selves'. All we can say for sure is that there is at any moment a collection of thoughts, feelings and actions connected with us here and now, and we can call this collection 'myself', or better 'one of my selves'. Avoid like the plague the illusion that you already 'know yourself' — because you don't!

Individuality

I prefer to reserve this word for the 'I' of the real man or woman into which we hope to be transformed. If we take our reality to be our 'will', that is, our power to choose and decide, then we can say that Individuality is a single permanent will. But it remains very hard to grasp or picture and is still harder to talk about.

Will

Few words are used so carelessly and with so little real content. 'Will' should stand for something special:

the power to make an act of one's own choosing. It is useless to try to pin down what we mean by an 'act' or by 'freedom' or 'choice'. It is almost impossible to get a clear picture of what 'will' stands for, and there is a good reason for this: that will is, like 'I', always the subject and never the object of experience. My personal conviction is that **will has the property of separating and joining together,** so that we can speak of 'fragments of will', or of 'united wills'. We are aware of conflicts within ourselves and it is not hard to see that these come from opposing 'wills'. It is not so easy to see what is meant by the unification of will, because this comes about only through the process of transformation. Anyhow, I shall use the word 'will' for any large or small power to choose and decide.

Mind

Some people say that the word mind stands for nothing at all. Others say that it is the awareness of what is going on in our bodies. Others again connect it with thinking and would say that where there is no thought there is no mind. I shall use the word 'mind' to stand for all that we can be aware of going on inside ourselves, but this is not a definition. We each of us must discover for ourselves what mind really is.

Soul

This is even more disputed than mind. Without going into details, I shall use the word 'soul' to mean a transformed and independent 'mind'. The soul is to the mind as a pot is to the clay from which it is fashioned and fired.

Sensation, Feeling and Thought

These words stand for different kinds of experience

that can arise in our minds. We shall learn how to recognize them in Chapter Five.

Consciousness

I shall take consciousness to be a kind of energy that 'lights up' our inner state in a way that is rather like electricity that 'lights up' a room. Just as electricity can do more than produce light, consciousness makes a variety of activities possible. For example, it is the chief means by which a direct contact can be made between two minds.

Hope, Love and Faith

These are operations of a still higher energy, that I call creativity. The point is that we cannot produce hope, love and faith by our own choice, in the way that we can, for example, produce thoughts or even feelings. It is even more important to realize that these great words are mostly used without any conception at all of what they really stand for. They are typical of 'inner world' operations that we can neither understand nor communicate until we have gone a long way along the path of transformation.

It is very useful to reflect upon these and other words of this series and ask ourselves if we can give them a meaning based upon what we actually experience and recognize. This exercise of 'self-questioning' has almost unlimited potentialities, and yet, like any other, it can be misused. We have to learn not to let our associations drift idly round a question and we must not allow ourselves to brood over things we cannot understand.

Right self-questioning is an **act of will**: it places us in front of our own ignorance at the very point where there is a chance of learning something new. Sincere self-questioning can be shared. It makes a special bond between those who try to penetrate into meanings, especially the meanings of the important elements of our inner life.

Memory

We must know our own memory. It is that which binds the fragments of our life into a coherent whole. But few people have coherent, total memories: they cannot remember all at once the different things that they remember sometimes.

Most important of all, **they cannot remember themselves.** One of the most useful exercises I ever learned was shown to us by Ouspensky in 1921. It consists in the struggle to remember one's own existence while one is engaged in any kind of activity. This exercise soon brings home to us the weakness of our memory. We deceive ourselves in supposing that we **can** remember what we want to remember, because we confuse the power of occasional recall with the ability to remember constantly.

A second very important exercise connected with memory is **the attempt to remember feeling states.** If we could remember grief in the midst of joy and joy in the midst of grief, we should be half way to inner freedom. But who has such a power of memory and how is it to be cultivated?

By examing such questions, we begin to understand . what a queer thing memory is and to see how far we are from a clear idea of what the word 'memory' really should mean.

Conscience

This immense word is 'understood' in such different ways as to have lost the power to influence us. We talk of a 'bad conscience' when what we mean is our reaction to some social pressure or to a habit formed in child-hood of regarding some form of behaviour as 'wrong'. Since such reactions are little more than the condition-ing of our emotional reflexes, they have rightly ceased to be regarded as sacred. We know equally well that a 'clear conscience' can mask indifference, self-satisfac-tion and complacency of the most devastating kind.

Can we find a meaning for 'conscience' which will always be the same for all people and restore the deep significance that this word had for our ancestors? Ouspensky defined conscience as the state in which one feels together all one's emotional contradictions. This 'awareness of contradiction' is certainly an important element, but it is not all that true conscience gives. Gurdjieff called it the most Sacred Impulse and the 'representative of the Creator' in man and that which alone entitles a man to be called a son of God. This definition is very far from the weak version of contem-porary psychology, which dismisses conscience as an emotional fixation. I am quite sure that it is nearer the mark to say that we all have a psychic instrument that knows the truth about ourselves. It is this instrument that is rightly to be called conscience. It is an incon-venient instrument for those who do not want to face the truth and they develop various protective devices that prevent its messages from reaching the conscious mind. Those who wish for transformation must both wish and be prepared to know the truth and for them the 'awakening of conscience' is a necessary step.

Sincerity

I have just used the phrase 'truth about ourselves'; but what is this truth and how can we recognize it? Like a computer, our thinking apparatus can work only by the rules that it is trained to follow, and it can use only the ideas that are fed into it. It is notorious that one man's 'truth' is another man's lie and that our capacity for being deceived — and for deceiving ourselves — is endless. Our feelings are even less reliable; indeed it is our **dislike** of unflattering truths that shuts our minds to them.

The remedy for our inability to accept the truth is the practice of sincerity or openness. This is a deceptive undertaking. We can mistake self-accusation or even self-loathing for sincerity, whereas they may be the very cloak behind which we hide the truth from ourselves. 'Sincerity' with others may be hypocrisy, insolence or officious interference in their affairs. There is a stupid sincerity which consists in saying unnecessary things or speaking at the wrong time to the wrong person. And yet sincerity is the key to conscience and the best means of establishing a deep relationship with those whose help we need. It is said that a pupil on the path of transformation must practise 'absolute sincerity' with his master. Such phrases are misleading for they suggest that ordinary people are able to be sincere. When groups are formed under the guidance of a person experienced in the way of transformation, they are given, at an appropriate moment, the 'task of sincerity'; that is, of giving an exactly truthful account of their own experience. The value of this exercise lies in demonstrating that sincerity is not achieved by the wish to be sincere, but by the attainment of inner freedom and the power of decision that comes with it.

Sincerity is a means for arriving at self-knowledge, for making true communication possible, and for the awakening of conscience. It must be practised with discretion and intelligence — always realizing that it can be counterfeited and that there is something in us that does not wish for sincerity. This 'something' must be brought into the **light** of conscience.

Attention

We know what it is to be attentive or inattentive; but do we know what attention **is** and what **makes** it come and go? The well-known exercise of attention — how long can you look at the second hand of a watch moving round without the slightest break in your attention? — will convince anyone that we cannot 'hold' our attention unbroken for more than a couple of minutes. We know that attention depends very much on interest: our attention is 'riveted' by an exciting drama whereas it soon wanders away from a dull task. If we are not 'paying' attention, a shock will 'bring us back', or perhaps for no apparent reason our attention returns and once again we are connected with what we are doing.

All this is common knowledge, but how little it is understood. Can we improve our power of attention? There are many exercises that can help, but they do not get to the root of the matter, which is the 'black-out' in our experience when attention goes and the corresponding 'light-up' when it returns. These have been compared with switching off and on again an electric light. The analogy suggests that attention is a flow of energy that starts and stops by itself. And yet our attention is so intimately connected with ourselves that we cannot accept the idea that we do not and cannot have any power over it. My personal conclusion is that **attention is an act of will** — the simplest and most primitive act of will that comes before we can do anything of our own choice. **We are our attention.**

Where our attention is, we are. When our attention goes, 'we' go.

This conclusion is, after all, only one of many possible explanations of attention. I have given it as a starting point for your own study. Whatever attention may or may not be, it is certainly important. It has something to do with energy — probably conscious energy — and it has something to do with will and therefore with 'I'. You should study it for yourselves and reach your own conclusion. Even if you have tried the exercise of watching the second hand, try it again and do your best to notice the way attention comes and goes.

Decision

This word seems easy enough to explain: a decision is an act of will. But when do we **really** decide? We should not use the word decision unless we are clear that the act of decision was really made. How often we say that we decided something when in reality we merely discovered that we were committed to a course of action, either by our own desire or because we were compelled. By using the word 'decision' carelessly in our own thinking and in our conversation with others, we overlook both the rarity of true decisions and their great importance. I shall try to use the word decision exclusively to mean **conscious acts of will in which we are aware of having chosen between two alternatives and of having committed ourselves uncompromisingly to carry the decision into effect.** It is very important to establish for ourselves this use of the word and to use other words like 'intention' or 'proposal' to signify acts of choice without firm commitment.

Presence

We need a word to convey the state in which 'we' are

present within 'ourselves'. We talk about being 'absent-minded' and about 'presence of mind', but we do not notice the peculiarity of a situation in which we can speak of 'me without I'. If we look upon 'me' as our home, we are bound to admit that we are seldom at home. We expect from ourselves and from others responsible behaviour that implies acts of will, when the 'I' is **not there to make** such acts.

Another way of looking at it is to say that 'we' can be **asleep** or **awake**. When we are asleep we cannot 'decide' and we are therefore not responsible. This is the stage of what Gurdjieff called the 'man-machine', who can only act as he is made and wound-up to act: that is, according to his automatic reflexes and the stimulus of external happenings.

Once one has grasped the distinction between presence and absence, it soon becomes obvious that we are seldom 'at home'. This must arouse in us the desire to be **able** to be present. I remember experiencing it as a very real but peculiar kind of fear. "If death should come on me at such a moment," I said to myself, "What would be left but a dead body? Where would I be?" Later, I discovered what a sense of security and freedom came from the awareness of presence and the realization that I did not lose contact with myself even when I was asleep.

I cannot explain or describe what 'presence' is, but I can say that it is not an exclusively mental state. It is linked to my bodily existence here and now, and yet it is not dependent upon it. It is more than being aware that one exists; it is like being aware that there is a substantial bond between 'I' and 'me'. This bond is, I personally am convinced, what is meant by 'soul'. The point is that we cannot do anything about our soul, but we can do a great deal about presence. Some of the most important spiritual exercises are for renewing and maintaining the state of presence.

Understanding

We need a word that is much stronger than 'knowing' to express the assurance that comes with experience of life and with reflection and reason, and that makes it possible for us to make our own decisions and if necessary to take decisions for others. I shall use the word 'understanding' with this tremendously strong and positive meaning. What we **understand** is an integral part of what we are. It cannot be taken from us. It has come from experience shaped by knowledge. It has been tested in the fire of life and we cannot doubt it. It has the "if I put my hand in the fire it will get burned" quality. Understanding is the 'eye of the will'; it enables us to act with assurance that cannot come from knowledge alone. New facts may contradict what I believe today to be reliable knowledge, but they will not destroy my understanding.

Knowledge is the content of my mind, but **understanding is the shape of my will**. My understanding is the possession of my 'I'. If anything that I have learned in this life will remain with me when I die, it will be my understanding — not my knowledge.*

Knowledge can be transmitted from one person to another, but not understanding. For example, a basic element of understanding can be expressed in the words: "never give up!" Plenty of people will agree that this is right, but very few understand what it means. In the last chapter I tried to convey what I understand by

---

*In his *Meetings with Remarkable Men* (p 240) Gurdjieff defines understanding as "the essence obtained from information intentionally learned and from all kinds of experiences personally experienced".

'sacrifice' and 'help', but no one who has not experienced these actions nor learned how to make them possible can understand their real significance. It is a very useful exercise to examine one's own understanding whenever one meets with a new idea or proposal for action. We cannot commit ourselves to what we do not understand; so that our understanding is the limit of our decisive acts of will.

Freedom

This is a peculiar word, because we cannot 'know' what freedom is. We cannot explain or describe it. We cannot even remember what it is like when it is not present. Consequently, we are always in a state of doubt as to whether the word freedom means anything at all. And yet we cannot get away from it, because the total absence of freedom would make nonsense of everything that matters to us.

The point about freedom is that it belongs to the world we are trying to reach — not the world in which we find ourselves. We are bound to see it upside down. We **think** of freedom as escape, release **from** constraint, **from** rules and laws that do not suit us. Real freedom is freedom **towards** the real world in which 'I' am no longer a stranger but have found my place where all that **I do** corresponds to what **I am**. We have an advantage here over the philosophers, who need to grasp ideas with their minds before they can accept them. Freedom is self-contradictory and cannot be grasped by the mind. It is a property of the will and it has no place in the mind anymore than in the body. To the mind, freedom looks like non-freedom and non-freedom looks like freedom. Only those who have tasted the reality can understand what this means.

107

I have devoted much space to the discussion of words that I regard as important for inner-world communication, not so much as to explain them as to suggest ways in which we can study them for ourselves. They cannot profitably be discussed in cold blood; that is, apart from the inner experiences to which they refer. The aim of group discussions should not be to talk about words but to share experiences. Out of this sharing the meaning of words emerges spontaneously and then people begin to understand one another. A link is forged between them that can never be broken.

3. UNSPOKEN COMMUNICATION

When all is said and done, the spoken word remains inadequate as an instrument of communication about inner world experiences. For the visible, tangible world of things and bodies, it works well and is the means whereby men can co-operate in dealing with it. Because it is successful in its own sphere, we ask too much of it and are disappointed when we find that for the things that really matter to us — our innermost longings and aspirations, our secret hopes and fears — it fails us miserably.

That which connects us in the visible world divides us in the invisible. We need a kind of **anti-language** that will work in the opposite way from that of speech. Speech is effective when it is clear and unambiguous. The anti-language must be imprecise and multivalued. It must convey its meanings by undertones and overtones. Ordinary communication must make itself heard and felt. The anti-language is spoken **sotto voce,** unnoticed except by those whose inner ear is opened.

I first became aware of this strange language when I was with Gurdjieff during the last two years of his life. Again and again, he told me things that were of deep and lasting importance, while his lips were telling comic stories about Englishmen and zeroes. I have described elsewhere the way in which twenty people sitting round the table could receive individual messages and be convinced that Gurdjieff had spoken to them alone.* This kind of communication requires that those who take part in it should be in a special state of sensitivity. It has the peculiar character of the anti-language I have been describing. The communication is strong and convincing and at the same time it is so elusive that one asks oneself if it is not hallucination.

It need not be intense and astonishing; most people will agree that there can be an unspoken recognition between two strangers whose eyes happen to meet and who will never speak a word, and yet know that something has passed between them. This suggests that we all must have an instrument for unspoken communication, but do not know how to use it.

I am sure that unspoken communication is possible and that the ability to use it can be developed and trained. One form is called **telepathy,** or the communication between minds at a distance. This is seldom in words, but in images and impressions. Two people discover that they often think of the same thing at the same time. When husband and wife are joined in a deep sympathetic union, this kind of telepathy is frequent and they even learn to rely upon it as a guide to action. It seldom progresses to the degree of two-way communication in which both parties are aware that a

---

*e.g. in *Is There Life on Earth*, J. G. Bennett, Stonehill, 1973, p. 100.

message has been transmitted, and must therefore be regarded as a relatively primitive stage.

Clairvoyance, or the ability to perceive events outside the field of immediate sense-perception, is probably less frequent than telepathy, but it certainly does occur. It can be developed by appropriate exercises. Some of the Sufi brotherhoods of Asia attach great importance to the development of non-verbal communication. I have lived for short periods with small groups of dervishes who claimed to be in communication with absent members and especially with their sheikh or guide. They assured me that anyone who has the capacity for spiritual development can acquire these powers if they are shown the appropriate exercises.

It is possible to conceal anti-language within ordinary language. I have described Gurdjieff's use of this method. It is possible in the written word.* I do not refer to 'hidden meanings': allegories and cryptograms — all of which work through the mind — but to a non-mental, non-verbal transmission by which there is a **contact of wills.** This is one of the great secrets of transformation: it is possible to achieve an extraordinary degree of co-operation, without visible communication, between those who have a direct contact of wills.

Another form of non-verbal communication is the **transmission of energy** from one person to another, or to many others. I have referred to this in connection with initiation and help. I can vouch for the reality of such communication from my own experience. One

*As the determined reader of Gurdjieff's *All and Everything* will eventually discover.

can be aware of the responses to a request for help from someone who is in a distant country. This kind of communication is not restricted in time any more than in place. One can learn to communicate with a source of help created in the past and to receive from it not only energy but even answers to specific questions.

All these possibilities exist because we men have instruments of perception and communication that do not depend on the five senses. These instruments remain latent and undeveloped under the conditions of modern education, which aims exclusively at preparing young people to deal with the visible and tangible world of sense perceptions. As far back as 1919 I became convinced that in Africa, at least, these inner instruments were known and trained. I learned about it from a remarkable man, Tracy Philipps, who had lived in Central Africa and had become close friends with several village chiefs who had developed these powers of communication and used them as a matter of course. It may be a great tragedy for mankind that the stampede to imitate European culture has overrun so much of the traditional techniques of communication. I believe it is wrong to suppose that these were used for 'black magic', except in rare cases: the striking instances personally vouched for by Tracy Philipps were wholly beneficent.

Mankind will regret the present emphasis on verbal communication and will be driven to seek again for the lost techniques. Fortunately much has been preserved and will be made available as the need for it becomes evident.

111

Friday, 6th November, 1953. DERA'A

"
Our car was invaded by a little Brazilian lady who explained loudly that she had paid for two front seats in order to be alone beside the driver. She has paid $1,000 for a trip of twenty-five days and lets everyone know it. On the journey she has done nothing but complain of the Arabs for not speaking English or French, of the country-side, of the talkativeness of our fellow passen-gers, of the slow driving of our excellent chauf-feur. She refused point-blank to allow the radio to be turned on. It has been interesting to watch how from start to finish it has not occurred to her that anyone matters except herself. "

JOURNEYS IN ISLAMIC COUNTRIES VOL. II

Chapter Four

SEEKING AND FINDING

1. AIMS AND PURPOSES

IF AT THE STATION I ask for a ticket, the clerk will say: "Where to?" If I reply: "Everywhere", he will shrug his shoulders and tell me to see a doctor. He may not realize that he is acting on the **Law of Selective Actualization,** which means that you cannot actualize all the possibilities open at a given moment. Even if we do not make the selection consciously, something will make it for us, and at the end of the journey we shall have reached some destination and all the other ones which were possible at the start will now be 'might-have-beens'.

We must grasp the significance of selective actualization, if we want to make the best use of our chances. When I was a young man, I found I had a gift for languages and learned a dozen or more without difficulty. I then began to study Chinese and I can vividly remember the moment when it was borne in on me that if I wanted to learn Chinese properly, I would have to abandon many other things I wanted to do. I gave up Chinese, saying to myself: "If I live to be a hundred, I shall never learn Chinese." About the same time I had the choice between going into politics and going to the East, and again I made my decision, realizing that it meant that I would never be a Cabinet Minister. I had, by that time, made up my mind that I wanted transformation more than anything else and was prepared to abandon other possibilities to achieve it.

113

There was, however, too much vagueness and too much imagination in my attitude towards transformation, and it was not until many years later that I began to see for myself what the selection really implied. When I made the choice, I was studying with P. D. Ouspensky, who insisted on the importance of clarifying our aim. He pointed out that we have no basis for deciding what is 'right' and what is 'wrong' for us. I cannot tell the booking clerk that he has given me the 'wrong' ticket unless I know where I want to go. Even if we say that there is an objective morality that makes some actions good and others bad: this affects me only if my aim is to be a 'good' man, or if I want to appear good in the eyes of my neighbours. If I have no aim: "God and the Devil are of no account."

Usually beginners on the path of transformation formulate their aims in terms far too lofty and too vague to give a basis of selection. We need to have some idea of the connection between aims and means. If we want to have a happy old age, it is almost certain that we must be prepared to work hard. If we want to be free, we must overcome our likes and dislikes. If we want to be healthy, we must keep our bodies in subjection. If we wish to acquire a soul, we must cultivate single-mindedness. If we aspire to perfection, we must be prepared to sacrifice everything that stands in the way, including ourselves. It is much better to select an aim that we can understand and be sure of than one which is no more than a pious hope.

The formulation of aim is the first test of sincerity. I have quoted the example of the lady who wanted to be free from herself — but could not sacrifice one tea cup. We constantly lie to ourselves about what we really want: but it is no use torturing oneself with self-accusation. If we cannot be sincere and want to be, then we can only say that this is an aim to be attained in the future. We cannot be sincere to order.

Nevertheless we must at least try to be clear about what we really want and try to decide if we are prepared to pay the price.

2. LINES OF WORK

Many people imagine that their aim is to 'help humanity' or to 'do the Will of God'. As they cannot know what humanity needs or what God's Will is, such aims are safe enough; but they are usually riddled with self-deception. Gurdjieff said: "If you want to be a good altruist you must first of all learn to be a good egoist." If we want to help others, we must first of all learn to help ourselves. The truth is that human nature is so constructed that neither egoism nor altruism can be achieved separately. We need others and they need us.

This is not the whole story. We may not know what 'God's Will' means; but we can be pretty sure that mankind exists to serve some purpose and that we cannot get very far if we ignore our own place in the 'scheme of things'. Just as egoism is limited in its scope, so also is the pursuit of a narrow and sectarian aim that would isolate a group from the rest of humanity. This is by no means obvious, nor acceptable to all, but if we start with the hope of transformation, we must suppose that there is a Great Purpose in our existence. Otherwise transformation would have no meaning.

From such considerations, we can reach the conclusion that an objectively sound aim in life must
combine three distinct objectives:

1. To perfect ourselves as far as possible.
2. To help others.
3. To serve the purpose of our existence.

Gurdjieff called these the 'Three Lines of Work'. I
do not know where the scheme originated, but during
the forty odd years since I first heard of it, I have
grown more and more convinced that it is the only
sound basis for planning one's life.

It is interesting to compare this scheme with the
'Three Disciplines' of the Shivapuri Baba, that together
make up what he called **Swadharma** or Right Living.

1. Bodily Discipline. Care of the body. Duty to oneself, one's family and the society to which one belongs.

2. Moral Discipline. Practice of the virtues incul-
cated in the *Bhagavad Gita*. Freeing oneself from the
slavery of like and dislike. The strengthening and
purification of the mind.

3. Spiritual Discipline. The search for Truth or God.
Meditation on ultimate Reality. Abandonment of all
attachments.

In this scheme, help to others and service occupy a
minor place. "Think of God alone! Put away every
thought from your mind" was the old man's sovereign
precept. I think that when we compare this with
Gurdjieff's three lines, we see where East and West
differ in their attitude to the aim of existence. The East
sees life as an evil from which we are to seek liberation.
The West sees it is the field in which we are to seek
fulfilment. The contradiction is striking, but it does
not follow that one is right and the other wrong. There
is very little difference in the selection of possibilities

that will be. made according to which scheme one adopts.

It is not one's philosophy of life that matters, but the way one carries that philosophy into practice. A philosophy of pure egoism consistently and intelligently followed out would lead to the realization that one's own good is inseparable from that of others and that neither we nor our neighbour can find enduring happiness that is not in harmony with the purpose of existence. At the other extreme, the 'search for God alone' will lead us to the discovery that God is to be found in ourselves and in our neighbour — not in some abstract **Nirvana** of the mind.

We men are endowed with a limited measure of **free creativity.** We have to serve a Great Purpose, but we can do so in part by self-fulfilment. We can choose a task to accomplish in life and once we have done so, we must treat it as a sacred obligation. It becomes for us a test of right and wrong. What helps us to accomplish our task is right for us and what hinders is wrong. The Shivapuri Baba called this a 'choice duty', i.e. a duty we lay on ourselves by our own choice. Gurdjieff called it a 'whim', and said that his whim was to bring men to a new understanding of God. Orage said that his whim was to edit the best literary journal in London. My whim is to demonstrate that it is possible to bring all possible human experience into 'a consistent scheme, and I have attempted it in *The Dramatic Universe.* It does not matter that one will fall miserably short of one's ambition: the point is that such aims or whims as these can be consistent with the three-fold scheme. It is even possible that a personal aim is a necessity, without which the 'Three Lines of Work' will not take shape as a way of life. The 'choice duty' may be simply that of

117

being a good wife or a good father, or of being a 'credit to one's profession'. All that is required is that it should be realistic and taken with the utmost seriousness as a 'sacred obligation'.

3. STAGES OF TRANSFORMATION

One of the aphorisms inscribed in the Study House of Gurdjieff's Institute for the Harmonious Development of Man was: "We can only create conditions for work, we cannot do your work for you." This was not to belittle the importance of conditions, but to emphasize the distinction between what others can do for us and what we must do for ourselves.

We could not even start if there were not evidences all about us that people before us have searched for and found ways of self-perfecting and so left for us the **image** of the Perfect Man. We are not drawn by abstract moral principles, but by the **Ideal** as incarnated in the heroes and saints of former times. It is from them that moral rules derive their authority, not the converse. We who are Christians accept the Christian ethic, not because it is logical or scientific, or because it has been proved to work well in practice — indeed many would say that the Christian ethic has been a dismal failure — but because we see it exemplified in the life and doings of Jesus and the apostles and saints who followed Him. In the same way Muslims, who are well aware that the ethic of the **Qur'an** does not apply in the conditions of modern life, are ready to accept Muhammad as the Perfect Man—**Insān-i Kāmil.** Buddhists see Him in Gotama Buddha, Jews in Abraham and Moses, Parsees in Zoroaster, Hindus in Rama or Krishna.

These figures are what Gurdjieff called '**Sacred Images**'. Round each of them we see a revealed doctrine and a way of life. What we do not see is that each of them is a Source from which there flows a stream of higher energies that make transformation possible for their followers. All men are influenced by these energies, even if they reject the Sacred Images from which they flow, and in this way the inner potential for transformation that exists in every man is given shape within their minds. This is the Ideal that calls to each one of us, and if the image of the Ideal Man arouses us to respond, we find ourselves embarked on the path of transformation.

This need not happen consciously. At the start there is bound to be much fantasy and self-deception, but if we look carefully, it is always the lure of the Ideal that gives a direction to our lives.

The next step is the transition from the general **condition** to a specific and particular **way**. We read or hear about some method. We are impressed by a person or group of people we may meet. We find a new set of conditions that makes it possible for us to learn, to struggle and to receive help. We are faced with the choice between following the path that has opened to us and holding on to the way of life that we have grown into. This may involve struggle and sacrifice. We are not close enough to the channel of transmission of knowledge and help to be able to make full use of our capacity for effort.

Many people get stuck in this stage because they lack the discrimination to distinguish between authentic teaching and artificial and unrealistic methods. It requires courage as well as discrimination to push the search further, because it will mean sacrifice of an unaccustomed kind. For example, it may require us to admit that we have made a mistake and to be ready to seek afresh, separating ourselves from others who cannot understand the cause of our dissatisfaction and will ascribe it to impatience, jealousy or wounded pride. The image of the Ideal must be very strong and clear if we are to make the next step.

If we persist, we may find ourselves in a new set of conditions where the pattern of opportunities corresponds to the pattern of our own nature. The action now becomes more specific and therefore more fruitful. We may be convinced that we have 'found our way' and that all that we need is to persist loyally in the path we have chosen. There are still pitfalls and it is not easy to recognize and avoid them. From my own experience, I would say that the hazards at this stage are chiefly the following:

1. Too much dependence upon a person before the true teacher-pupil relationship has been established. This relationship belongs to the next stage, but far too often the seeker imagines that he has not only found his 'true' teacher, but also that he has been accepted as a pupil. The truth is that, at the stage of general teaching — the **exoteric** stage as it is sometimes called — there is no personal responsibility either towards the teacher or towards the seekers.

2. Methods that are too limited in their scope and too rigidly applied. Failure to understand that no technique is of universal validity and that the results it will give depend upon the stage reached by the seeker and the suitability of the conditions. A method may for a time give encouraging, even astonishing results and arouse conviction in the mind of the seeker that it is the one and only right method for him. After a time, it will

cease to give results and the seeker will very often be told that this is his own fault — because he has not tried hard enough or he has spoiled his work by lack of loyalty and persistence. He may recognize the considerable truth in such admonitions and yet fail to see that he **cannot** try harder and that the doubts that he is told to suppress are legitimate consequences of his own discrimination.

3. Inability or unwillingness to sacrifice something that stands in the way. This may range from the material sacrifice of possessions to the subtlest sacrifice of self-will or self-love. If the first stage has developed normally, the seeker will have acquired enough insight into his own nature and weaknesses to recognize his attachments and to understand why the sacrifice is required. This hazard arises when the seeker has found the path that is right for him and stands before the possibility of forging the pupil-teacher bond and yet fails to make the very step that will allow the teacher to help him. The teacher is often forced to appear to be making an unreasonable demand or to be losing interest in the seeker. Disappointment and resentment may blind the seeker to the opportunity that lies in front of him.

It is characteristic of the upside-downness of the path of transformation that when the seeker is ready to blame himself and feels obliged to persist in spite of failure, he should probably move into a new environment; whereas, when he feels that the blame lies with the teacher and that he himself is being misunderstood, it is probable that he should sacrifice his own feelings and submit himself unreservedly to what is required of him.

The fourth stage is, I believe, marked chiefly by **the kind of help** that the seeker can receive. To understand this, we must return to the notion of a **Source.** Energy can flow from a source, but it must have a channel or it will be dissipated and lost. The channels for psychic energies are people. Such people are rightly called **Initiates.** They are not necessarily perfected men or women and they may make mistakes and even lose their way; but because they have allowed a specific action to occur in them, they have become channels for transmitting higher energies which can help the transformation of others.

There are dozens of ways in which the channels of transmission can operate. I have met with several and each one is different. This is one of the characteristics of the fourth stage: there is no longer a stereotyped recognizable pattern. All is beautifully ordered and effective, but **it is always specific to a particular time, place and set of circumstances.** When these change, the pattern dissolves.

I will give an innocuous example. Once, travelling in North West Persia, we met a Sufi Community of the Jellali Order, whose main centre is in Turkestan. We were welcomed and I could not doubt that they had the authentic quality of a 'channel' of transmission and were engaged in a specific task. Circumstances prevented us from staying long enough to make a real contact but, in subsequent years, several of my friends whom I had told of the meeting tried to find them again, but they had vanished without trace. Later, I heard that they were connected with a very widely spread brotherhood in the Middle East in which quite unexpectedly I became interested and from whom I received very valuable help.

One point of the story is that such opportunities are made available at a particular time and place and must be taken in the particular way required. Once the moment has passed, the door is closed or, rather, it ceases to exist. A second point is that, to recognize the opportunity, one must have reached the stage in one's own awakening at which help can be given. These are not theoretical or abstract principles: I have seen again and again how close people have been to a wonderful step forward and have missed their chance. Often these very people have been convinced that they were ready to make any 'reasonable sacrifice' to make a real step forward and yet **could not see** that what was required of them was not only reasonable, but obviously necessary for their own good.

This is not to say that the demands made upon us when we enter the fourth stage are easy to foresee or prepare for. On the contrary, they are always unexpected and even contrary to what we had been taught to look for. In Chapter Two, I referred to the Law of Hazard. Our ordinary 'understanding' takes hazard as something to be avoided by care and foresight. **In reality it is overcome only by taking more risks.** Help seldom consists in making things easier, but rather in creating what seem to be gratuitous and even absurd difficulties. We lean on a crutch and it is taken away in order to make us walk. We put our trust in a person and he betrays us to teach us to trust ourselves. We have 'tested and proved for ourselves' that some method or technique is reliable and helps us to progress: we are told that it is an impediment to be discarded. If in each case we can find the right response, we discover that the 'unreasonable' demand was exactly the right way to give us help. This is not hard to grasp once one has seen the working of the law of hazard. Only the interaction of conflicting processes can break the vicious circle of repeating what is no longer serving any purpose. At the fourth stage, everything is new and unrehearsed and the 'creation of conditions' is a special art which no one can master without the help of a very high energy.

I shall not attempt to describe any of the further stages because once the fourth is passed, the process is completely individualized and no general account has any value. I have been very fortunate in meeting several men and women who have gone beyond the fourth stage of transformation and have seen for myself that they were all completely different. Ordinary people are more or less alike. Even those who have reached the fourth stage fall into distinct categories or types which, though relatively small in number, allow of some degree of generalization. For this reason, 'schools' of the fourth degree select their pupils to allow for the most effective combination of types. Beyond this stage, no such rules apply. The further a person advances towards perfection, the more does he become **himself** — unique and individual. He has a task to perform that he and he alone has the necessary qualities to accomplish. If such people become known as Saints or Sages, their uniqueness is overlooked and they are remembered as idealized images conforming to patterns that ordinary people can recognize and emulate. No one but those closest to them can know who or what they really were.

4. GUIDANCE AND PROGRESS

We all want to improve ourselves in some way or another: even if the 'improvement' does not amount to transformation as I have described it. We all, therefore, need knowledge and perhaps help and advice. We may hope to get the knowledge from books or by listening to lectures, but when it comes to help and guidance, we need an actual person. What kind of person is likely to be an expert in what we want to learn, and how are we to find him? We shall find various degress of expertness among professional psychologists, and also among theologians and philosophers, but I assume that we are looking for something that none of these is likely to provide. We want an expert in the methods of self-development or transformation. If we lived in the East, we could find Hindu Gurus, Muslim Sheikhs, Buddhist Bhikkus; but we also know that the great majority of these have only very limited repertoires and fulfil much the same function as the parish priests of former centuries in Europe. Some come to the West with a reputation for saintliness, wisdom or magical powers, and acquire a corresponding following, but how are we to know if they can give us what we need?

What **do** we need? Let us suppose that we have read several books and are sufficiently interested to have tried some method described, or practised some form of meditation recommended in one of these books. This will almost certainly have brought us to the point of realizing that something is missing. We made an encouraging start and then got stuck. Having written a number of books on these subjects myself, and being known as a 'pupil of Gurdjieff', or a 'member of Subud', or a 'devotee of the Shivapuri Baba', or a 'follower of Sufism', I receive letters from all over the world from people who, for the most part, want me to tell them how to find a teacher or the way to be initiated in one of these paths. In a way, this book is a general answer to such letters and to others which have never got themselves written.

The first advice I would give to anyone is to ask himself what he is really looking for. If he wants someone else to take his decisions for him and to relieve him of responsibility he should look for a professional in such matters — a psychologist or a priest — according to his preference for scientific advice or religious advice. It would be unwise to go to an unqualified person not subject to a code of conduct laid down by a professional body or a church. There are too many men and women without either real experience or an understanding of the gravity of the task of taking decisions for others. The true teacher or spiritual guide is concerned to help others to learn how to take their own decisions and accept their own responsibilities.

If the proposed 'teacher' claims to represent a tradition or a doctrine, then this should be studied. If it takes away responsibility and asks for blind acceptance or trust in a person, then I would strongly counsel the seeker to be wary. Only strong people with a well-developed sense of discrimination can take risks of that kind. Remember that you are still at the first stage: you have not enough experience to take any kind of commitment. You do not know yourself or your true needs and you have very little to guide you in deciding whether a particular person or group of people can help you. If you try something, make yourself a promise that it will not be for more than six months. This is long enough for you to form some kind of opinion. It may be that a probationary period will be demanded of you. Do not jib at this: on the contrary, welcome it as a means of finding out all you can without being committed. Do not waste a moment. I have often seen people treat the period of probation as a waste of time and not think of themselves as having 'started' until it is over.

Even if no probationary period is demanded, the seeker himself should fix it — I have suggested six months. There is a fundamental reason for fixing a limited time for any operation: it is connected with the Law of Hazard. Any 'timeless' process will lose direction unless consciously regulated. A definite period ensures that an independent factor will be introduced: namely the fresh decision. This must, as far as you are able, be a **true decision.** You must understand that you are free and are making a free choice. If you decide not to commit yourself further, break away altogether and try again elsewhere: the experience will be of great value.

The seriousness of such free acts of choice is not sufficiently appreciated in our modern world where we live in the midst of conditioning, and the very aim of our society seems to be to remove from people responsibility for their lives and acts. **The way of transformation must be the exact opposite of this.** Whatever else it may lead to, it must make us into free, responsible individuals, able to direct our own lives in accordance with the greatest objective good.

When the moment of commitment — still provisional and limited in time — does come and we are going to accept a person or group of people to guide us: what are we to look for? We must not expect a perfected man, fully enlightened and wholly disinterested. Such people have tasks more serious than teaching beginners. Moreover, according to my belief, even the highest and most perfect Guide or Teacher is fallible: the whole existing Universe is riddled through and through with hazard and uncertainty. We must hold fast to this principle, or we shall get into trouble by expecting from a person, who may be manifestly superior in wisdom, power and goodness, a degree of infallibility in judgment and action which is contrary to the universal law of hazard. In other words, we must remember at all costs to allow for the mistakes and short-comings that we are sure to find in our teachers.

This may seem to contradict the principle that one must trust one's teacher and be prepared to do whatever he requires. This principle is connected with sacrifice and help: it is not an universal law. We must be prepared to sacrifice our self-will and we must learn to 'allow ourselves to be helped'. We must do all this without reservation and yet with our eyes open.

At the second stage, we must be satisfied if we can learn methods that are useful to us and are placed in circumstances that help us to know more about ourselves. Even this requires a degree of commitment that may not be easy to accept. We are too accustomed to letting ourselves be pushed around and yet never deciding to submit voluntarily to discipline for the sake of gaining strength.

It is very important to remember that **time is measured.** The second stage must not take long. Far too many people are content to go on learning the same things or using the same techniques long after they have served their purpose. In my opinion, three years is the longest that one should allow for this stage. If we find that we have not come to a very specific and personal action in this time, there is something wrong. Either we have been too passive, or the environment does not suit us. It may be very pleasant and encouraging; we may have made good friends and feel that we are doing useful work. None of these things will carry us into the third stage, unless the four factors: learning, struggle, sacrifice and help are unmistakably at work.

Unfortunately, we are seldom able to find, at the right moment, the right conditions to make a step ahead. We may be compelled to wait; but we must not stagnate. The responsibility is our own and no one else's. We cannot expect from the teacher or from the group what they are not competent to give. They may most sincerely believe that the methods they transmit provide all that is required and yet everything may be moving in a circle, getting nowhere. I have seen so much of this that I can write about it with feeling. The illusion of progress is created by the reality of the struggle. The pupil is made to work hard at impossible tasks and feels satisfaction due to the conscious energy evolved in the struggle.

Another kind of self-deception comes from learning. There are groups that devote themselves to the study of esoteric matters, drawing upon the almost limitless resources of the various traditions. Such studies are useful only to the extent that they open channels in the mind and allow new forms of communication to develop. If this is not grasped, study becomes an end in itself and those engaged on it go round and round in a circle getting nowhere and yet convinced that their learning will give them power.

A third pitfall is connected with initiation. There are in the world at this time many groups and brotherhoods that possess the secret of some form of initiation; that is, the transmission of help through contact, or some ceremony or ritual. One may be, like Subud, contact with one of the Universal Energies. Another, like the Spiritual Regeneration movement, may make

129

use of special **mantra** or phrases for repetition. I refer here only to actions that I believe to be perfectly genuine and beneficial, and not to any of the more dubious magical initiations involving secrecy and often sexual contact. The genuine initiation systems are necessarily restricted in scope. They do not, in themselves, transmit knowledge nor do they provide for the organization of struggle. Often they repudiate the very idea of sacrifice as unnecessary for those who have received initiation. The result, here again, is that the action begins to repeat itself, producing the illusion of progress because those who practise it sincerely feel better for it and can observe an improvement in health, emotional stability or the removal of defects. What they do not notice is that there is no real transformation, except for the very few who find the way to combine struggle and sacrifice within the framework of the particular initiation they have chosen.

Finally, there are movements almost exclusively based on sacrifice. The leader of one such, for example, claiming to be an incarnation of Deity, requires of his followers the wholesale sacrifice of possessions and complete devotion to his person. This also can so absorb the interest of the devotees that they do not observe that they have become dependent upon the relationship with the master and, since this cannot progress, they do not progress either.

The point is that all these movements may be good and honourable. The methods and techniques are genuine and effective. Each one attracts certain types of people who respond to that particular approach. But the trouble is that they tend to fix people in their own characteristics rather than enable them to get free from themselves. They are useful for a time — that is why I have suggested a time-limit of three years. There is a terrible waste of potential, because tens of thousands of excellent men and women all over the world are tied up in groups and movements from which they derived real benefit at first, but which, out of mistaken loyalty or perhaps simple ignorance of the laws of transformation, they continue to follow years after the transforming process has come to a stop.

It is obvious that a different kind of expert knowledge and skill is required to enable the transition to be made from one stage to another. The **guide** who can create the situation needed for personal transformation of the fourth stage must be altogether more versatile than the **teacher** who can produce third stage conditions. In a sense, the demand creates the supply. There are times — and the present is one of them — when the world needs transformed people more abundantly than usual, and at such times **guides** or 'higher teachers' are sent out from the centres which can prepare them. But there must also be a demand on the part of those capable of being helped. It is not the business of a guide to convince people that they need him: this they should discover for themselves. Only thus can they be ready to take the commitments that are required at the fourth and later stages.

So far I have referred only to teachers and guides who are directly concerned in transmitting teaching and help. There are also what I should call 'Spiritual Directors', who do not teach or organize groups or lead movements. They are wise, experienced and saintly men who are channels for the transmission of the **Unitive Energy** (E2) and can therefore do an immense amount of good in the world, usually without being recognized for what they really are. I have met two or three such men in my life and the debt I owe them is immense. Yet I have never been connected with them as pupil with teacher or 'belonged' to the spiritual order of which they were members.

In searching for the pattern of our lives, we must take into account the extreme complexity of the invisible society of transformed people and people in process of transformation. I have called these* the **Psychoteleios** and **Psychokinetic** Groups. There are many good and legitimate ways, all forming part of this complex structure. Often the members, and even the leaders, of the various groups are not aware how necessary they all are. There are stupid jealousies that seem to be the cause of great waste and effort. In reality, the tensions and conflicts are necessary means of overcoming the Law of Hazard. Anything too well and too neatly organized sows the seeds of its own destruction. There is a very high wisdom that knows how to use chaos for creation and how to bring harmony out of conflict. We must be careful not to criticize what we cannot possibly understand.

The more we move along the path of transformation, the more evident does it become that our puny wisdom and our modern science fall very far short of being able to understand how human history is being directed. Nevertheless, we all have our place in it and we should never be satisfied until we have found it — and **know** that we have found it.

---

*In *The Dramatic Universe* Vol III Ch 41

"
One evening, Major Pinder, a former British Intelligence officer who had met Gurdjieff in Tiflis in 1919, and who, knowing Russian very well, acted as his interpreter, announced that there was to be a lecture.

We all went to the Study House as usual, but instead of practising the exercises sat expectantly round the hall on our cushions.

Time passed: ten o'clock, eleven o'clock, midnight.

At last Gurdjieff arrived — evidently having driven out from Paris — accompanied by Madame Ostrowska, Madame Ouspensky and Major Pinder. He stood and looked at us all for a long time and said in English: "Patience is the Mother of Will. If you have not a mother, how can you be born?" He then walked out of the Study House.   "

WITNESS

Chapter Five

THE BODY AND ITS NEEDS

1. RIGHT ATTITUDE TO THE BODY

WE CAN MAKE A CONSIDERABLE step towards the goal of our existence — whether we picture it as perfection or freedom or lasting happiness or the fulfilment of our destiny — if we establish once and for all the right relationship to the physical body. We must look upon it as an instrument to be used, an animal to be trained, a slave to be commanded and yet treated with due regard to its dignity and its rights. If we have not already acquired this attitude, we need to exercise ourselves in it until it is established.

"This body is not 'I'."

"It is not myself."

"It is a thing that will degenerate if not cared for."

"It is an animal that will disobey if it is not disciplined."

"It is mine for a short time only and during this time, I must make the fullest use of it."

"In all things, at all times, it must obey me. I can and will be its master."

By meditating on such notions as these, we establish the right mental attitude. But the connection between mind and body must be forged by discipline.

It is good to accustom this body to hard physical work. We should endeavour to acquire a rich repertoire of bodily skills.

We must observe the weaknesses of the body. One person sleeps too much, another overeats, another

135

dreads physical pain. These weaknesses must be overcome. They should be overcome in childhood. If, to our misfortune, we have not learned to discipline our bodies in youth we must not think it is too late. We must start where we can. Opportunities will come: through illness and accident we can learn that physical pain can be used for self-mastery. We can set ourselves to overcome useless or harmful physical habits.

If I have ever found that some habit was getting hold of me, I have set myself to break it and I am certain beyond all doubt that this practice has brought me health and happiness as well as a most precious freedom. Probably, if I had disciplined my body more than I have, I would have benefited still more: and looking back, I can see that during periods of self-indulgence in bodily matters, I have lost ground and have had to pay for it.

It may seem that I am advocating an austere asceticism. This is certainly not the way I have lived my own life and I see no reason for recommending it to anyone who does not feel convinced that it is right and necessary for him. Our body should be treated like a servant whom we love and trust. We can and should attend to its needs and from time to time indulge it in what it enjoys. But, first and foremost, it is necessary to establish the relationship of servant to master.

It is by no means hard to keep a right relationship to this body, once one has discovered the 'taste' of it. It has certain surprising characteristics. It is not necessary to struggle with a reasonably well-disciplined body. It will do what is asked of it almost before we realize what is needed. This is because the perceptions of the body are much faster than those of the mind. For example, I may be feeling lazy and make up my mind to sit and read rather than do some necessary job. The next thing I notice is that my body has got up and is doing what is required, while my mind is still day-dreaming.

2. RELAXATION

Though primarily an action in the physical body, relaxation is a technique with almost unlimited potentiality. According to Gurdjieff, there are seven degrees of relaxation, starting with 'letting go' the tensions in the voluntary muscles and leading through deeper and deeper 'giving way' of nerves, feelings, thoughts, desires to culminate in the final and irrevocable abandonment of self. In this chapter, I shall not go beyond exercises that produce deep relaxation of the body, and allow free flow of the psychic energies.

It is easy to obtain a relaxed state of the body by hard physical work, by skilful massage, sauna baths and similar means. These are all useful, but they do not produce the deep relaxation that we are looking for. **For this, we must learn how to make a direct connection between our will and the part of the body we wish to relax.** I used to call this merely 'working with attention', but I have since discovered that it is much more interesting and important. I have already explained that the conscious energy can be directly connected with our will — that is our 'I'. This energy has power over the sensitive energy and can be made to control the states of the body. Learning to relax is thus a first step towards the voluntary control over physiological and psychological processes that are usually thought to be outside the power of our will. Usually, we are content to rely upon the established reflexes and trained reactions, so that if I say, "I will lift my arm and let it fall again", the required movements do occur, but not under the direct control of my will.

It is well-known that yogis and other 'holy men' of the East can acquire the power to stop their breathing or their pulse, to concentrate their blood in a given part of the body and so produce swellings and many other weird effects. All these are obtained by learning how to use the conscious energy in the way I have described. Such psychic tricks are of no special interest to us: but deep relaxation certainly is, because it is the way to control states that we need to be able to produce when required.

There are many ways of producing deep relaxation by conscious energy. I shall now describe one that works well for most people. Start by taking a comfortable sitting posture, with the spine as straight and erect as you can make it without straining. You can support your back at the base of the spine. Verify that your head is freely balanced on your shoulders and that there are no obvious tensions. Rest your hands palm downwards on your knees. Now — become strongly aware of your eyes as if 'you' had entered into them and were experiencing the sensation of being present in your eyes. You can now relax your eyes and all the muscles surrounding them. Keep them open or you will fall asleep when you relax deeply, but you should now be seeing without focussing on any object. To avoid strain, lower but do not close the eyelids. Move your awareness over your face, into your mouth, to your throat and successively *wish* each part to relax. Pass on from the throat to the back of the neck — where you should feel yourself present in the muscles of the neck — and move your awareness down the right arm, penetrating into the muscles all the way to the finger tips. The same with the left shoulder and arm. Then return to the throat and let your awareness travel through the thorax down to the diaphragm. Here comes the familiar 'awareness of the navel' which is so often treated as a joke. It is very far from comic, because there is in this region a concentration of the vegetative energy which must relax. It is necessary to spend several minutes relaxing the abdominal muscles and obtaining a deep rhythmical breathing. The awareness is again made to travel into the right thigh and down the right leg. This must be done slowly enough to make sure that there is a real contact between 'you' and 'your leg'. The same is repeated for the left side.

Once this is completed there should be a general sensation of the mass of the body and a coherence of awareness of your own presence within the body. The whole exercise is then repeated; but with the determination to penetrate more deeply into the nerves and blood vessels. This causes a tingling or vibrating sensation followed by a feeling of the 'wholeness' of the body. The exercise is continued for as long as one can keep from falling asleep or losing the thread of what one is doing. It is not easy and it may have to be done twenty or thirty times before one can be sure what is meant by 'contact with the body'. It should never be done more than once a day. Once one has learned how it is done, the time taken can be reduced.

There are many variants of this relaxation exercise, but so far as I can ascertain, all of them require to be done by concentrating conscious energy. This cannot be done by an effort: on the contrary any kind of force makes relaxation almost impossible. It is purely a matter of skill. This skill is a special kind of struggle: it is hard work — very hard indeed to go really deep — and yet it must not be forced. Any forcing is bound to produce tension and defeat its object. This illustrates the importance of **understanding** what we are about. The aim of relaxation is to allow a free flow of the vital and psychic energies. Deep relaxation goes further and enables the creative energy to work in us and to organize the mind and transform it into soul. We cannot accomplish this transformation by the energies that are more or less under the control of the mind, and so we must **allow** the work to be done in us. Those who practise deep relaxation — sometimes also called deep meditation — become aware of this working and learn to co-operate with it.

3. DIET AND FASTING

The state of the sensitive energy is certainly influenced by what we eat and how we eat. Moderation in eating is undoubtedly a wise rule. The eastern custom of eating meagrely at most times and enjoying occasionally an enormous feast is to be preferred to slight but constant over-eating.

I am not so sure about the value of a specialized diet. About thirty years ago, I adopted the vegetarian diet for a year. As a result, so far as I can tell, I became weak and ill, recovering completely when I resumed eating meat. All the same, I believe that meat should be eaten sparingly to keep good health and control over the psychic energies. Drinking wine and spirits to excess is obviously harmful. I have lived in Muslim communities where no alcoholic drink was ever seen and have felt very well. Nevertheless, I must say that I would not wish to follow a way of life that prohibits all alcohol. I was very much taken aback when I last saw Pak Subuh's remarkable eldest daughter Rochanawati in Athens in 1960 and she advised me to give up drinking as it would shorten my life.

There is something here that requires to be understood: even the smallest quantity of alcohol disturbs the balance of the nervous system. With Gurdjieff we were expected to drink heavily when required by him to do so; but this was a very special situation. His long meals, preceded by an hour or more of reading aloud, in a crowded room and thick atmosphere, were not conducive to alert attention. This was made far harder by having to drink armagnac or vodka to each of the Idiot Toasts that were invariably proposed at every meal. Gurdjieff would tell the same stories over and over again or exasperate new-comers with his strange behaviour. And yet, at any moment, without change in voice or manner, he might tell us something that we would not have missed for worlds and tell it in such a way that it could be understood only at that particular moment. In order not to miss such chances, we had to make superhuman efforts to keep an alert attention and after a time we realized that alcohol played an indispensable part in the experience. Its effect is to open channels that are normally obstructed and so enable the 'Essence' to take over from the 'personality'. It is obvious that alcohol used in this way is a powerful instrument for self-knowledge and self-change. It produces similar results when drunk indiscriminately, but we do not know how to get the benefit from them. Once again, we cannot say if alcohol is good or bad unless we are clear what it is we want from it.

Another way of opening channels in the mind is to reduce the bodily activity by fasting. There are several kinds of fast. The old Christian custom of abstaining from flesh and food on Fridays is no more than a relic of Jewish discipline and a reminder of the sacrifice of Good Friday. The Muslim fast of the month of **Ramazan** consists in abstaining from all food and drink from sunrise to sunset. The stated aim is to give all believers the experience of hunger so that they can feel compassion for those who are starving for want of the means to buy food. Prolonged fasting has a different effect — it purifies the blood and regenerates the psyche in a very remarkable way. I have experimented to some extent with fasting and have found that it has many advantages. Fasting completely — drinking only water — for several days enables one to pass over a barrier and experience a wonderful freedom from one's body and clarity of mind. I have always followed Gurdjieff's advice to do at least one hour's hard physical work during every day of fasting. He explained that the digestive enzymes are then consumed by taking up blood sugar, failing which they tend to poison our mental state. In the early years at Coombe Springs — 1946-1952 — short but complete fasts were part of the programme of our summer seminars. Most people disliked them intensely, but agreed that the results after two days fully repaid the suffering of the first 48 hours.

Somewhat later, I tried for my personal benefit the practice of a weekly fast of thirty-six hours from Sunday to Tuesday. I never liked it and even after seven or eight months I could not overcome my dislike. I always felt weak and my mind would not work properly, but by Wednesday I always felt wonderful, and extremely active mentally and physically. I never observed any kind of harm from fasting and during the time I was practising it regularly — about a year and a half — my inner vision was opened and I saw things that changed my outlook on life. I can, therefore, recommend it to anyone who is prepared to undergo a certain amount of discomfort for the sake of sharpening his mental powers.

All this is very mild. I have never tried prolonged fasting — that is for more than a week — I think chiefly because I have always been too busy to reorganize my life to allow time for it. In 1962, we had a remarkable visitor at Coombe Springs, Hasan Tahsin Bey, who when we first met in 1920 was Chief of Police for Istanbul. He was a Bektashi Dervish and a great exponent of prolonged fasting. While he was with us — it was the bitterly cold winter of '62-63 when the snow lay on the ground for ten weeks — he fasted for two periods of 20 and 25 days, eating only a few raw apples and a handful of snow. Although well over eighty years old, he worked hard in the snow for the first fifteen days. After 20 days, his strength was obviously failing and he abandoned the project of fasting for forty days and forty nights with great reluctance. He explained to us that anyone who accomplished this 'canonical fast' attained complete and final liberation here in this present life. He had tried several times, but had never completed it. He was evidently bitterly disappointed that his love of fasting had not communicated itself to the community at Coombe Springs and soon afterwards returned to Holland. We have not heard of him since.

Regarding diet in general, I will end by reproducing a well-known tradition of the Prophet Muhammad.

The King of Persia, hearing of his achievement in abolishing idolatry among his followers and learning that there were no physicians in Arabia, became concerned and sent two of his most skilled physicians to take care of the Prophet and his companions. After several months, the physicians asked to see Muhammad and complained that they had never been consulted. The Prophet invited them to examine all his companions and they found no trace of illness and went back in wonderment to ask how this was possible in so unhealthy a climate. Muhammad replied that his followers had adopted his advice to eat in such a way that they always rose from the table with their hunger unsatisfied. This was the reason why they were never sick.

I am sure the advice is good: but I myself have seldom followed it strictly — I do, however, try to hold to the rule of never eating more than I am sure my body wants. I can say for myself that it is thirty years since I have ever experienced any kind of digestive or similar inconvenience.

4. POSTURE — HATHA YOGA

A reasonably obedient body is not necessarily an efficient or well-trained body. Most people, walk, stand, and sit badly. They have unnecessary bodily tensions and nervous movements — fidgeting — all of which waste energy. Bad postures have a harmful effect on the breathing and the circulation of the blood. It is certainly worthwhile learning about these things and about ways of correcting the defects. F. M. Alexander's book *The Use of the Self* contains much valuable advice and his pupils and followers in many parts of the world give lessons in the right use of the body. I have seen enough of this work to recommend it, and, of course, they are not the only specialists in this field. Expert advice and instruction are very desirable, but they need not be given by a teacher of transformation. F. M. Alexander claimed to be materialistic in his philosophy and rejected any suggestion that his method had any objective other than the efficient functioning of the organism, and yet it has helped many seekers on the path of transformation. We should go to the best specialist available whenever we need specialized advice. I have known followers of a 'spiritual' teacher refuse to seek help outside the 'teaching' from the mistaken idea that this would show disloyalty or lack of trust. Only a very poor teacher would allow his pupils to believe that he knew everything. It is strange that in scientific matters no one expects a man to be expert outside his field and yet it is almost an article of faith that a true spiritual master must be expert in everything.

The concentration of conscious energy in the body can be facilitated by assuming various postures influencing the state of the nervous system and the circulation of the blood. These methods are well-known in India under the name of **Hatha Yoga,** but there are many variants outside of Hindu tradition.

I think it is useful for anyone to practise some of the simpler postures, if only because of their value in giving one confidence in dealing with one's body.

The Buddhist monks have an attitude towards posture which differs from that of the Hindu Yogis. They recommend a 'stable and easy' posture with crossed legs as an aid to meditation. At first this posture is by no means easy for Europeans accustomed to sitting on chairs, but there is no question that it does help in keeping the mind steady. This illustrates an important principle, namely, that the state of any part of the organism influences the state of every other part. We are accustomed to sit in habitual postures — or rather non-postures — and our thoughts become linked to them. When we need to think in a non-habitual way, we should change our posture, otherwise the habit of the body will bring out the associated reflexes in the brain. If you observe the conditions in which original and interesting thoughts have come to you, you will probably find that you were not sitting in a habitual posture at the time.

The Sufis have special postures for their spiritual exercises. The commonest consists in sitting on the floor on the left leg with the arms clasping the right knee.

5. RHYTHMIC AND RITUAL MOVEMENTS

So far as I know, Gurdjieff is the one great 'Teacher of Temple Dancing' who has come to the West. I first saw a display of his exercises in 1920 and I saw him teach classes in Paris up to a week or two before he died in 1949. Of all that he taught, there is little doubt that the greatest appeal was in his remarkable, almost end-less variety of exercises or 'movements' with the accompanying music. He claimed to have spent a quarter of a century travelling through Europe, Africa and especially Asia in search of the secrets of the temple dances and the methods of training and expres-sion taught by the traditional schools.

Like relaxation, ritual dances work on all levels. The first stage is to achieve body-consciousness. Movements that are made automatically and unconsciously may be skilful and even graceful, but they have no potential for transformation. Gurdjieff and others have described the long slow process by which temple dancers of Central Asia acquire absolute rhythmic precision of gesture and movement, by becoming conscious of the subtle harmony of the basic postures from which ritual movements are built up. Such perfection is required only from those who intend to devote themselves to temple dancing as the central theme of their self-realization. It is, however, useless to attempt anything in this field unless postures, gestures and transition movements are made by a direct contact — through conscious energy — between the will and the body.

The same aim is served by the entirely different procedures of executing very difficult and complicated movements and of overcoming fatigue and pain by continuing an exacting rhythm for as long as the body can bear.

The harmony of the instinctive-motor, emotional and intellectual centres is achieved through dances and rituals that are at the same time expressive of emotional states and universal laws. Gurdjieff had an amazing repertory of such movements and they have been successfully developed by his principal exponent in this field, Madame Jeanne de Salzmann.

At a deeper level, ritual dances and movements are used to provide a channel for the flow of creative energy. These are easily misunderstood because of the connection between the creative energy and the sexual life. What may appear to the onlooker to be orgiastic self-indulgence may in reality be a highly controlled

147

liberation of creative energy, not for the enjoyment of ecstatic experience, but for the awakening of the soul.

The best known example of this is the **Derv** or turning ritual of the Mevlevi or Whirling Dervishes. I first witnessed their ritual in 1919, when the Mevlevi Order of Sufis was still in the ascendant in the last days of the Ottoman Empire and the great ones of the land were not only proud to be members of the Order, but took an active part in the ritual dance every Thursday evening. I could see for myself that there was no question of uncontrolled ecstasy; but certainly those who were adepts entered into conscious communication with an unseen world. One of the Sufis, who took it upon himself to instruct me, explained that the purpose of the ritual was to detach the soul from the body and so become aware of the state into which it would enter after death. He added that the certainty of immortality in Paradise engendered by this exercise accounted for the reckless courage shown by the dervishes in battle.

I have witnessed — as most readers will have done — many demonstrations of Indian, Chinese, Japanese, African and other ritual dances and rhythmic movements. I am doubtful whether any of those that I have seen were directed towards controlling the flow of conscious energy and liberating the soul-stuff from its dependence on the body. It is, of course, legitimate to allow spectators to see at least some of the rituals but public performances are incompatible with the complete detachment that the participants must maintain.

Ritual movements can be used for many purposes besides the development of the body and its powers.

There are regular daily actions such as the Moslem obligatory prayer requiring fifty or more prostrations every day. Special postures such as kneeling, sitting on the heels, sitting cross-legged or in the lotus position, are all designed to help in maintaining attention during prayer and meditation. The abandonment of these traditional practices has left a void into which many bad habits can penetrate.

A special case is that of ritual ablution as a preliminary to any kind of spiritual exercise. I referred in Chapter Two to the importance of the skin and the need to keep this organ in a state of maximum activity. I think it is probably true that the sensitive energy becomes contaminated by the activity of the day and by any strong emotional or sexual experience and is eliminated from the body through the skin. I do not remember where I heard this explanation; but it accounts well for what I have observed. Our skin — particularly the sensitive and exposed parts — is coated with this rejected energy which is removed by rubbing with cold water. This, as I was told, is the original reason for ritual ablutions enjoined in religion. Other customs, that now appear to be superstitious survivals, probably had equally sound reasons which were known to those who introduced them.

Apart from such routine practices, which anyone can learn, work on postures and rhythms requires expert teaching and such teachers are hard to find in any part of the world. There is, unfortunately, a tendency to treat the expert knowledge as esoteric and those who have it are often reluctant to share it outside their own select circle. This not only restricts opportunities for those who could benefit. — and would be prepared to work hard — but has a second less obvious drawback. This is the tendency for those who learn special dances and movements — without intending to become professional temple dancers — to continue to work at them long after they have ceased to have a progressive or transformative action. Gurdjieff concentrated great efforts on teaching his system of movements and ritual dances during the years 1918-1924 and 1924-1929. In both periods his aim was primarily to prepare teachers and demonstrators and only to a secondary degree to teach the method to students. This has probably led to the mistaken idea that intensive work on such exercises can with profit be continued indefinitely. Madame Ouspensky, one of his most loyal pupils, who introduced the method to her husband's group in England about 1933, stipulated that no one should work at the movements for more than two years. I have heard that in Sufic communities exercises connected with development of bodily powers are practised intensively for a year at most and afterwards used only for renewal. If this is correct, it would seem very desirable that those who are able to teach rhythmic movements and ritual dances should open their classes widely so that the largest possible number should benefit.

6. THE STOP EXERCISE

The Mevlevi Dervish ritual or **mukabele** consists of three parts. The first is a mental preparation carried out in a seated posture. This consists in a **zikr** or repetition of the unitive invocation or simply of one of the Names of God. It is followed by a procession in front of the Sheikh to the accompaniment of music.

The **Sema Hane** or Hall of Audition is adjacent to the tombs of the most revered sheikhs and saints of the monastery and each dervish as he passes stops and bows very low before continuing. Then comes a signal, which may be loud and sharp or scarcely noticeable, from the musicians and all the dervishes on the floor of the Sema Hane freeze in their places. Everything is deadly silent.

The music resumes with a strong rhythm and then the well-known turning movement begins. It was explained to me that the **stop** signal symbolizes the moment of death when the soul becomes aware of the Truth. This 'moment of truth' is said to reveal the whole of one's past life and the dervish is required to look at himself as if he had just died and his power of choice were taken away from him. The **derv** or turning movement which follows represents the bliss of paradise when the soul enters the new dimension of 'circularity'.

A few months after I had witnessed the Mevlevi **mukabele,** I was invited by Gurdjieff to see a class of pupils who were learning his 'temple dancing'. Once again, I witnessed the 'stop' but in quite a different form, as the pupils were made to rush across the floor and freeze in mid-motion. Some stopped dead, others tumbled over and remained stiff and still where they were. Gurdjieff gave no explanation at the time.

Several years later, I not only saw but participated in the stop exercise at his Institute for the Harmonious Development of Man at Fontainebleau. We were then instructed to use the 'stop' to observe our posture, thoughts, and feelings, without allowing any inner or outer movement. I was able to ask Gurdjieff, who spoke Turkish well at that time, whether the aim of his

151

stop was the same as that of the Mevlevis: to give the seeker the taste of separation from the physical body. He assured me that this was the case, but that in Central Asia the uses of the stop exercise were graded according to the pupils' ability. I had been told, he said, the inner meaning of the exercise only because I was not participating. For those who were being trained, there were different inner exercises that they had to learn and practise during the 'moment of truth'.

Some thirty years after these experiences and conversations, I began to teach Gurdjieff's rhythmic exercises to my own pupils at Coombe Springs and also used the 'Stop Exercise', in the way he had explained it, during their physical work in the grounds. From my own experience, I can say that this exercise has a very powerful effect not only upon those who are being trained, but also upon the teacher. It must not be undertaken except under conditions which allow the energy it liberates to be used rightly. For this reason, there is a widely accepted rule that no one may use the stop exercise without the authority of a guide of the fourth degree.

7. 'WORKING FROM WITHIN'

I have taken as the title of this section a phrase I used in *Concerning Subud* to distinguish an action produced without any conscious effort on our own part from exercises based upon struggle or intention. The Subud **Latihan** is a remarkable example of this kind of action. It is initiated by the 'opening' or 'contact' given by a helper or initiate and all that it requires is a responsive passivity or better, permissiveness, on the part of the person receiving the contact. I have no doubt at all that something does pass between those giving and those receiving the contact and also that the action is reciprocal: that is to say, something passes in both directions. According to Pak Subuh's explanation, the contact is made with the Great Life Force or energy — **Daja Hidup Besar** — that is, the quickening power of Almighty God. The reciprocal action is the release of contaminated energies — impurities — from the one who is opened. I must say that my experience of being present at thousands of openings — often as the only helper present — agrees with the explanation. There is a great force at work and it does indeed release or drive out 'something' from the person opened. This 'something' may be so unpleasant as to cause the helper to vomit or feel abysmally wretched. It may also be light, beautiful, and wholly delightful.

At first, I was prepared to accept the possibility that the action of Subud latihan was wholly spiritual and beneficient but the experience of more than ten years has demonstrated that the situation is much more complicated than this. Some people benefited from the very beginning and after many years continue to benefit, others — and I am one of them — gained immensely from the latihan for two or three years and then began to suffer ill effects. In my own case, these ill effects were loss of initiative, bad health and extreme fatigue, coupled with a sense of neglecting my real duty in life. Others had very powerful experiences that captivated them, but soon got into trouble. Many became psychiatric cases and far too many committed suicide. Yet another large group experienced little or nothing and soon abandoned the latihan. Finally, there have been a large number who gained positively, but after a few years ceased to experience anything and lost interest, continuing to practise the latihan occasionally and finally stopping altogether.

In my opinion, the conclusion to be drawn from these observations is that without discrimination, actions which 'work from within' are not to be recommended. Indeed, they require a greater degree of experienced guidance than exercises that depend upon voluntary effort.

It remains to explain why I have included the Subud latihan among the 'needs of the body'. The reason is that the action takes place, in the early stages at least, in and through the physical body. There are spontaneous movements of all kinds: dancing, singing, shouting and gesticulation, as well as various strange and interesting postures spontaneously taken by the participants. The greater part of the beneficial results reported concern the bodily organism; improvements in health, the cessation of undesirable bodily habits, and unmistakable 'rejuvenation'. It is much harder to say whether the Subud latihan produces favourable and progressive changes in the mind and soul. I am fairly sure that my own mental powers suffered during the time that I practised the latihan regularly and so far as I can judge, I would say that it has been the same with most others.

These observations may suggest a very unfavourable verdict on my experience with the Subud latihan since I first met it in 1956. I can only reaffirm that I am quite sure that I benefited and have continued to benefit. The explanation seems to me fairly obvious: the spontaneous action of the latihan — the working from within — does not differ from any other kind of exercise in being beneficial when it is done at the right time by a person at a suitable degree of development, and its benefit continues only for a limited time. If persisted in beyond this time, the action either ceases or becomes harmful.

The trouble is that there are three determinants:

1. Selecting the right people to be opened at the right stage of their development.
2. Finding the right time and conditions for them to be opened.
3. Recognizing the moment when they should stop and go on to some other experience or combine the latihan with some other form of work.

All three require specialized understanding which no one, including Pak Subuh himself, appears to possess. This is not said to belittle the remarkable achievements of Subud throughout the world or to disparage its founder. Pak Subuh is unique among all the people I have met, in the simplicity and completeness of his faith. He believes that he has been entrusted with a mission for the Good of Humanity and he has devoted himself unsparingly to this mission for forty years. He is, in addition, a most lovable and intelligent man and rightly commands the devotion of thousands of followers all over the world.

8. BREATHING EXERCISES

I have left these to the penultimate section of this chapter because, though respiration is an activity of the organism, the breath is the carrier of the higher energies of sensitivity and consciousness. Breathing exercises, therefore, are not strictly speaking bodily exercises.

There is, however, one misconception that should be corrected here. It is rightly said that breathing exercises can be dangerous and should never be practised without expert guidance. This is true as applied to exercises involving a change in the rhythm and character of breathing from what is normal. Most people, however, do not breathe normally and they are in need of exercises to help them. Poor breathing weakens the body and can even shorten the life. Breathing and posture are closely connected. One should be conscious of the vertebral column and learn how to recognize the free flow of energy that comes from a good posture. One should also recognize the benefit of deep and rhythmic breathing in which the entire capacity of the lungs is brought into play. We too readily assume that because some organic function is normally controlled by unconscious instincts, the same function cannot, or at any rate should not, be brought into our mental awareness. It is useful to be aware of our breathing and verify that it continues to be free, deep and rhythmical. These attributes of the respiration are necessary for health and they are a valuable preparation for the exercises in which breath feeds higher energies into the psyche.

The body is furnished with reservoirs of psychic energy. Gurdjieff called them 'accumulators'. They are probably connected with the endocrine glands and the nerve ganglia called Chakras in the Hindu terminology. We draw upon these accumulators for every kind of psychic activity: instinctive, motor, sensory, emotional, intellectual and sexual.

9. SEX AND THE GREAT ACCUMULATOR

I am convinced that sexual energy is a species of creative energy, and that this is why it occupies such an extraordinary place in human life and influences all our activities. If sex were an exclusively physiological function, there would be no reason for it to be associated with psychic experiences and to play so great a part in man's creative work. We need consider it here only as it affects our bodies and their potentialities.

Physiologists have shown that the hormones exert a dominating influence over the chemistry of the blood and hence over all the functions of the body. Gurdjieff told us that the sexual glands are the great accumulators of psychic energy and that when any centre becomes connected with this central reservoir, its working is magnified several hundred fold. In some of the paths of transformation, the seeker is given exercises and tasks that lead directly to the opening of the reservoir of sexual energy, on the grounds that once the flow of the creative energy in any form can be regulated voluntarily, all other functions can be brought under control.

I have never had direct contact with such ways; but as far back as 1923, I had the experience of the opening of the Great Accumulator and of the extraordinary power over oneself that this gives. I have since had several opportunities of studying the ways in which this opening can be achieved. I have also observed the disastrous consequences of doing this artificially and prematurely. The first time I saw this was when I was sixteen years old at school in Godesberg on the Rhein, where the pupils were encouraged to drink heavily to prepare themselves for the excesses of Bonn University as it was before the 1914 war. An American fellow pupil drank himself into a state of delerium tremens and ten strong young men were unable to restrain him.

157

The superhuman physical strength that he displayed made a lasting impression on me. The next time I saw a similar effect was during the 1914 war when a mortally wounded man with his stomach shot away attacked the German Army with demonic energy.

The liberation of creative energy by violent experiences produces results similar to those of sexual intercourse. There is no value in such uncontrollable states. I have seen a man cut off — apparently beyond repair — from his spiritual potentialities by combining sexual intercourse and drugs in order to reach a particularly intense state of consciousness. All such things are to be avoided like the plague by anyone who retains the hope of reaching a real state of existence.

This leaves open the question of sexual activity as a bodily function. The question is constantly asked whether sexual abstinence is beneficial, or perhaps even necessary for those seeking perfection in transformation. In the Christian tradition the celibate state is regarded as more conducive to spirituality than the married state, providing of course that it does not result in strain or abnormality. In Islam, the contrary belief is held. The great saints of Islam were all married, as the great saints of Christianity were all celibate.

Faced with such contradictory evidences, what are we to conclude? The common element is the agreement that the sexual act is sacred and must never be prostituted to self-indulgence. The truth is that the sexual act, like all others, is governed by the conditions of time, place and person. There can be no general rule governing sexual behaviour that does not allow things that are sometimes harmful and forbid things that are sometimes right and even necessary. People vary enormously in all aspects of their sexual natures and no rigid moral or social rules can be just to all. Nevertheless, restraints are necessary, especially for what I have called* the **Dependent** group of society who cannot take their own decisions.

My own view is that there are four stages in the transformation of the sexual life of man and woman. The first is the stage of **immaturity** when good habits should be acquired by submission to discipline. There is much need of advice for young people; but, unfortunately, it cannot be given in any fixed formula. The key is discrimination, and advice and discipline are useful only as stepping stones towards discrimination. The present book is not concerned with the preparatory age, but with adult life, so I shall add no more.

The second stage is that of **expansion.** The sexual life opens — or should open — spontaneously and innocently. The young man or young woman cannot yet know how to regulate sexual activity — unless he or she is fortunate enough to have acquired discrimination at an early age — and rules are necessary. The sovereign rule is respect for the sexual act as the release of the sacred, creative energy — man's noblest possession. If this one rule can be communicated and accepted from inner conviction, the second stage of sexual development can go forward with complete freedom.

The third stage implies a combination of discrimination and experience. The seeker has acquired self-knowledge, the power of self-observation. He can begin to **regulate** his sexual life according to the results it gives. I am referring here solely to the organic aspect of sex: that is, the activation of the sexual organs, which is normally obtained by sexual intercourse of man and

---

**cf. The Dramatic Universe*, Vol III, p. 236

---

woman. The psychological and personal aspects of sex belong elsewhere.* The regulation of the physical act is a matter of self-discipline; but it is also — as I suggested in an earlier chapter — a very important form of sacrifice. The man or the woman who is able to give wholly and unselfishly in the sexual act and yet can experience the ecstasy of creative freedom, is ready to pass to the fourth stage of its development. The sexual act is peculiar insofar as it must be spontaneous and yet intentional in order to correspond to the nature or will-pattern of the person involved. Normality is a mark of sexual maturity.

The fourth stage is marked by understanding of the true significance of the sexual act. Its structure is in depth: that is to say it is **integrated** at all the levels of human experience. At this stage, the physical act is integrated with the fusion of soul-stuff and the union of wills.

I hope that I have succeeded in conveying my conviction that our bodily organism is a noble and wonderful instrument and that it plays an essential part in our inner transformation as well as in our outward life. We should learn to love our body as the dependent part of our nature. It cannot be a responsible being and it must never be allowed to dominate the rational part, that is our mind.

I believe that there is a stage in our transformation when the body accepts its true rôle and allows the energy of consciousness, which is not a bodily energy, to act in it. This results in a regeneration of the body

*cf. Sex, J. G. Bettett, C.S.P. 1975

that I have called elsewhere* the **resurrection** of the body in the midst of its terrestrial existence. There is a special kind of joy that accompanies this change. The Shivapuri Baba described it as **Sukha,** one of the three legitimate aims of our existence. If I am right in believing that I know what **Sukha** is, then I would add that it is not a permanent condition that, once gained, cannot be lost; but rather a marvellous indicator of 'rightness'. Its presence is a sign that one has taken the right care of one's body. Its absence is a warning that something has been neglected. **Sukha** is like **organic conscience** that enables us to discriminate with certainty between what is good for the body, and hence for the whole of us, and what is bad for it. It is probable that what Gurdjieff called 'organic shame' is the state of being sensitive to the presence or absence of **Sukha.**

---

*in *Concerning Subud* ch. 7

> " *I am sure that there can be a deep education of the character. It is not so much a question of change as of transformation. The same trait can be positive or negative. For example, there is true pride and there is false pride. We should be proud that we are called to be sons of God, but it is false pride and wickedness to ascribe to ourselves qualities that we do not have. True pride is the same as humility.* "

A SPIRITUAL PSYCHOLOGY

Chapter 6

HARMONIOUS DEVELOPMENT

1. HOW MAN IS CONSTRUCTED

ONE OF THE MISTAKES made by those who seek transformation is to suppose that the process can start for them as soon as they find the right method or the right teacher. This might be approximately true if we had lived our lives normally from the moment of our conception up to the time that we decide that we must seek for our Ideal outside our existing conditions of life. Unfortunately, no life corresponds to its destined pattern and we all have much to put right before we can safely make a start.

If we want to improve the working of a complicated piece of machinery we need to know how it is put together and what purposes all the different parts serve. We also need to have a means of recognizing defects and of diagnosing the causes of inefficient working. Man is the most complicated organization we shall ever meet with in our lives and we must know all we can about this organization if we are to improve its working.

In the present chapter, I shall examine some of the main defects of human nature that must be corrected in order to achieve harmonious development, and show how by studying them we get to know ourselves and by struggling with them we can acquire strength.

We must start by distinguishing what we are from what we have acquired. We must learn to distinguish

163

between what we are born with and what has come to us by the influence of our environment. The distinction needs to be made clearer and more explicit. We are not born ready made, but with a complex pattern of potentialities to be realized in the course of our lives. This pattern consists of three parts: independently, formed and developed.

First, we have a bodily organism formed by heredity and developed by a natural process, like that of any other animal. This organism has a marvellous anatomical structure and physiological dynamism. We cannot know it as a specialist would, but we can know enough to study its working. This depends largely upon a characteristic blood chemistry and structure of the nervous system and brain which we can change only to a limited extent, and then at grave risk of causing damage. This profoundly influences the ways in which we are able to see, hear, think and feel; that is to say all the states and processes of our mental life. We cannot separate ourselves from our ancestry and the hereditary make-up we have received from our parents.

Second, we have our own private share of the human **mind-stuff;** According to the view which I have worked out elsewhere* in some detail there is a great reservoir of sensitive energy partly enriched by conscious, and perhaps even creative, energy derived from the past experience of the human race. I call this the 'Soul-Stuff-Pool' and believe that there is a vast and continual recycling of this material. It enters at the moment of conception to produce the 'mind-stuff' of the new human being. This explains why there can be mental aptitudes and weaknesses and even memories in the

---

*in Vol III of *The Dramatic Universe* Ch. 40 p 167 ff.

mind of a child that cannot be accounted for by heredity. I think it is very probable that the share or 'quantum' of mind-stuff received depends upon the exact location in space and time of the moments of conception and birth, and that this is the reason why it is possible to predict some of the characteristics of a person by working out his or her horoscope.

Third, each human being has a definite and unique **pattern of will.** This pattern is his or her Individuality and it determines the way in which the 'I' in each one of us is able to act successfully. Our will-pattern settles our **destiny,** that is: the role in life that we are best fitted to play and the one that will give us the greatest measure of fulfilment. Of the three parts, the third is the most truly **our** reality, but it cannot act or even be aware of itself without the mind and the body. The will is the power to choose, but the exercise of this power depends upon the mind. I explained in the second chapter my conviction that the connection between the will and the mind is made by the **conscious energy,** and becomes permanent when we acquire a **soul.** Until then, the will depends entirely upon the accidental combinations that connect it with different parts of the mind. Sometimes it connects with thought, at others with feeling and at others again with the instinctive-motor centre. Later in the present chapter, I will describe ways in which all these connections can be studied and verified for ourselves.

The three parts — body, mind and will — are born together and they make up our **essence.** They lack experience: that is, the content of memory, and at first only the instinctive mechanisms necessary for life: breathing, eating and the rest, are already developed. All the rest must be gradually acquired by contact with the environment. The chief means are imitation and repetition. These are supplemented by the intentional actions of teaching and training from older people.

There is no guarantee that anything acquired from the environment will correspond to the natural tendencies and inclinations of the mind-stuff or to the pattern of the will. Indeed, it is so improbable that the the three patterns will fit together that we invariably develop a **personality** that does not correspond to what we really are. This means that the will has to use an instrument that does not suit its powers and that the mind cannot develop its full potentialities. This is why I wrote at the beginning of this section that, before the process of transformation can safely be undertaken, we must first put right the disharmony that exists between the four different parts of our nature: body, mind, will and personality. The easiest of these to change is the personality, because it is not inborn but, as it were, grafted on to us by outside influences.

2. SELF-OBSERVATION AND SELF-STUDY

Moral teaching and discipline tell us what we ought to do, but they tell us neither why nor how. This is the chief reason why modern man has revolted against general moral rules and has looked for some more convincing way of life. In the last section I have given, as shortly as I could, my own picture of how we are formed out of four distinct parts. This picture is not just a 'form of language' to help me to express what I meant to say. We greatly need to have as clear a picture as possible of **who and what we really are. I** myself am quite clear and confident that we are formed of four parts, though of course the idea of a soul-stuff-pool cannot be directly verified. The point is, that the division of mind, soul, will and personality **can** be verified. Its main value to us consists in that we can both verify it and use it to do something to put the situation right.

'Mind' is a vague all-purpose word like 'body'; but at least we learn how the body is constructed and what the different limbs and organs do for us. There is no reason why we should be ignorant about our minds, because we have available the means for studying them in the form of self-observation.

The first point to grasp is that **observing** oneself is quite different from thinking about oneself. We do too much thinking, even brooding, about ourselves and our problems. This gets us no further that brooding over a toothache. We have to learn how to **look** at ourselves from inside. It is best to start with one's body.

Practise the observation of postures, gestures, habits of movement. Do not be satisfied until you have **seen** something. You suspect that you slouch when you are seated, or fidget with your hands, or that you cannot look at a person steadily when you are speaking. Set yourself to find out how things really are, not just sometimes, but all the time that you are in that kind of situation. You have an 'inner eye' that sees from inside. At present it works involuntarily when something gives you a shock. You must learn to use this inner eye as skilfully as you use your outer eyes.

The words 'inner eye' may confuse you. You can call it an 'inner sense' or simply 'self-observation'. The great thing is to grasp that it works by **direct perception.** Just as you can see a tree or a table when you focus your outer eyes on them, you are able to perceive what is happening in your body when you focus your inner sense on it.

As soon as you have grasped what the inner sense is and how it works, focus it on your feeling states. The first step is to learn to distinguish between relaxed peaceful feelings and tense agitated feelings. It is not so important to observe **what** you are feeling as to be able to recognize **how** you are feeling. Learn to do this objectively, make up your mind to see **how** things are, before you try to change them. There is always a tendency to react automatically to any discomfort by trying to relieve it. This tendency is the chief reason why our power of inner vision has failed to develop. It is not comfortable to observe oneself as one really is and we either stop looking or we quickly make a change. This dissipates the energy that is released by perception. If we can bear to see ourselves and go on seeing, the conscious energy begins to concentrate and our will has the chance of doing something about it far more effectively than our usual mechanical reactions.

The hardest part of the mind to observe objectively is the thinking centre. We have flashes when we can 'see' our thoughts, as separate from ourselves; but we cannot hold on to this state of perceptiveness, to see how our thinking brain works. Once we have recognized what the 'inner sense' is, we can practise ourselves in its use. We then find that our thinking is far from 'intentional' and also that we have very little control over it.

When we have learned to keep the different parts of the mind under the observation of our inner sense, we can begin to observe our personal characteristics. Self-study consists in **seeing, recognizing and remembering** the ways in which our mind works. Two things are to be avoided. One is 'brooding', or taking to heart what we happen to observe. We must know the facts, pleasant or unpleasant. The second pitfall is hasty attempts to change what we don't like in ourselves. The mind is an interconnected structure and if we change it in one part, we shall affect all the other parts. For example, we may observe that we have a tendency to leave small tasks unfinished and, seeing that this results in much waste of time and opportunity, we set our-selves to 'remove' this defect. We may even succeed in doing so, but this may strengthen another tendency of interfering in other people's concerns. This tendency remained harmless so long as we ourselves were easy-going; but our success in learning to finish off our jobs may be marred by our turning into intolerable busy-bodies.

This does not mean that struggle with bad habits is useless or even harmful. On the contrary, we can scarcely ever observe any mental activity unless we struggle with it. Struggle brings the conscious energy that makes 'inner seeing' possible. Struggle consists in checking the manifestation of some mental process, and this is quite different from eradicating the tendency to it.

3. THREE BASIC ILLUSIONS

As if the natural obstacles in the path of transforma-tion were not enough, we are obstructed and confused by false notions about our condition. From the accounts preserved in sacred writings of the trials and tribula-tions of mankind two, four or even six thousand years before the present, two salient facts emerge. The first is that man has always suffered from delusions as to his true situation and the second is that the form taken by these delusions has changed from age to age. It seems as if man cannot help deceiving himself, but with increasing experience — that we call 'science' and 'history' — each set of illusions collapses only to be replaced by another set equally as absurd. We call the illusions of former ages by such names as 'primitive ignorance' or 'superstition' and pride ourselves on having destroyed them, not noticing that we have invented another set of our own.

The basic illusion of modern man consists in grossly over-rating the stage of development he has reached. This illusion takes three forms.

1. **The illusion of Unity.** We imagine that we have a single, undivided will and that whenever we say 'I' we refer to this one permanent will.

2. **The illusion of Consciousness.** We imagine that we are or can be aware at all times of whom we are and what we are doing.

3. **The illusion of Effectiveness.** We imagine that we can do what we choose to do and therefore are responsible beings capable of taking decisions and carrying them to a conclusion.

These illusions were characteristic of the **Magalanthropic Epoch*** that began about 500 B.C. and ended in the 19th Century. In the twentieth century they have been challenged by psychologists first and at this time by the great majority of young people throughout the world. Nevertheless, they continue to dominate all our attitudes. We demand of others what they cannot possibly give: responsible, consistent behaviour. We imagine that when enterprises are successful, it is

---

*cf. *The Dramatic Universe*, Vol. IV, p. 327 ff.

because those controlling them have acted effectively and responsibly. We are able to deceive ourselves into supposing that the advance of natural science is giving us 'control' over nature. We are now in a period of transition to a New Epoch; when, no doubt, new illusions will arise to replace the old. We can already discern the emergence of the illusion of irresponsibility, which leads people to imagine that they can have what they want without paying the price. This illusion is relatively new and it is a source of astonishment to those who look for historic precedents.

The main point for us to examine with the utmost seriousness is the assertion that **mankind lives in a state of perpetual illusion,** and if we begin to suspect that this assertion has too much truth in it to be pleasant, we should turn towards ourselves to verify or disprove it. If we have acquired some power of self-observation, we should be able to see that we constantly treat ourselves and others as if we were united, conscious and effective beings. Even when we fail dismally in some undertaking, we do not ascribe it to the basic illusions; but to bad luck and the malevolence of others, or at the most to lack of care or insufficient effort or intelligence on our own part.

The tendency to accept any explanation of human failures rather than admit the basic state of delusion is very significant. Once we have grasped it and seen how universal and how strong the hold of illusion is upon people, we can begin to understand both the necessity for transformation and also why it cannot begin aright until we have sorted ourselves out.

It is useful to combine self-questioning with self-observation in order to come to grips with the basic illusions. "Who am I?" "Am I the same at this moment as I was a minute ago? An hour ago? Yesterday? Last year?" "If I am my will, can I say that I always will the same ends?" "What part does will play in my daily life?" "Is my behaviour consistent with the belief that I am always the same person?"

"Do I recognize what consciousness really is?" "If so, can I say that I can be conscious when I choose?" "Can I remain conscious?" "If so, for how long?" "Can I remember myself?" "Must I accept that I am in reality asleep nearly all the time, even when I think I am awake?"

"Am I an effective being?" "Am I deceiving myself when I suppose that I do what I intend to do?" "Am I not the slave of my mechanical rôles — compelled to succeed in what I do well mechanically, bound to fail in what I cannot do well mechanically?"

"If I fancy myself as an effective person, can I sincerely affirm that I do what I intend to do?"

Self-questioning is an exacting discipline; and, unless it is taken seriously, it is worse than useless. One must never take for granted that one already knows the answer to a question; but on the contrary be quite sure that there are depths in it that one cannot yet expect to reach.

The way of working that I learned from Gurdjieff, and that I can recommend, is to choose a question, write it on a piece of paper and carry it with you everywhere you go. "Treat it as your God," said Gurdjieff, "Make it the most important thing in your life." "Take it out and read it again and again. Make yourself think about it with the determination that the answer must communicate itself to your will. It is not enough — though necessary — to take it into your mind. Continue for one week, not longer, and let a few weeks go by before you take another question in the same way."

Since I first heard of these illusions from P. D. Ouspensky more than forty-five years ago, I have met hundreds of people who have been attracted by these ideas, especially by their 'stark realism', and have embarked with enthusiasm or determination on the task of 'finding the truth for themselves'. But very, very few of these have genuinely seen the situation and freed themselves from the basic illusions. Probably the hardest of the three to accept is that 'we cannot do'. Even behavioural psychologists and proponents of the ultra-materialistic doctrine that man like everything else that exists is a machine and that free-will is non-existent — even they speak and act as if they and the people they deal with can and do act consciously and intentionally. It is no small achievement to free oneself from these illusions, but to have done so is to have gained a most precious freedom and peace of mind. It is hard to realize how much of human misery comes from the illusion that man is more evolved than he really is.

4. THE FOUR SELVES

The illusion of unity includes the mistake of supposing that we can speak of 'myself' in the singular. In this section, I am going to describe my own conclusions about the self-hood of man and how it can be studied. It is interesting that hardly anything on the subject is to be found in Western literature or in any Christian teaching about man. Apparently it did not occur to the Greeks to question the unity of man and Western psychology has built upon this omission the false notion of the human soul as one and indivisible. We are brought up to think that, simply because we have one body and one name, we are also one person. The Hindus call this the **Nāmarūpa** (name and form) illusion and claim to be free from it. And yet the doctrine of reincarnation, especially in its Hindu form, would imply that there is one 'self' that lives dies and is born again times without number until this one immortal self attains final liberation from **Samsāra,** the cycle of existence. Orthodox Islamic teaching also treats man as a self to be rewarded or punished as an individual.

Far more realistic accounts of man's nature are to be found in the Buddhist psychology, in Sufism and in central Asian beliefs, all of which were, no doubt, closely connected in their origins. According to these views, the human psyche is composite, being made of several distinct selves or souls. After many years' study of these doctrines and especially with the help of Gurdjieff's teaching and what I learned from Subud, I finally came to the conclusion that all men are composed of four distinct selves.

The selves are patterns in the mind-stuff. They have their own memories, habits, points of view and their own values, that is, what they take as important and unimportant. They are passive until the will enters into them, when they take charge of what we happen to be doing and change it according to their own desires or habits. We can think of them as puppets that come on the stage and play their part when the actor takes the strings in his hand.

I have called the four selves: the Material Self, the Reactional Self, the Divided Self and the True Self. I recommend the reader to study the following descriptions and then by observation of himself and others, by comparison and reflection, to decide for himself whether or not he finds the scheme useful for his understanding and if so, to get into the way of observing which of his four selves is in charge in any given situation.

1. The Material Self

This begins to take shape in the mind-stuff soon after birth as a young child makes contact with the material objects of his environment. The mind builds up the necessary behaviour patterns and these coalesce to form a self which is directed towards the material world, and takes this to be the only reality. It has no values, because these come with experiences of the emotional and intellectual centres that are not awakened in the young child.

The most important achievement of the material self is speech, which the child acquires by contact with the sights, sounds and other sensations of the material world. We should study our language and see for ourselves how it is based on material objects, so that even when we wish to speak about mental processes and states, we must make use of words and expressions that are taken from the material world.

The material self is the instrument by which we deal with the material world. It acquires a variety of skills, particularly those of hand and eye, but it also has an instinctive tendency to clutch and **hold on** to the objects with which it has to work. As the capacity for emotional feeling begins to grow, this tendency leads it to rely on material things and become attached to them. The importance of material objects is real enough; but attachment to them produces a set of values based on acquisition and possession. The material self begins to look upon success in dealing with the material world as an end in itself.

This 'materialization of values', can lead to very undesirable results. The material self claims the status of the true self. The will becomes attached to it and the further development of the self-hood is obstructed. This can be a real disaster, because by its formation the material self is without sensitivity to the feelings of others. In extreme cases it can be brutally callous in pursuit of material aims and regard the possession of wealth as the highest good.

We should, therefore, examine ourselves and learn to recognize the material self, which of necessity is present in all of us, for it is our main contact with the outside world, and see what place it occupies. Attachment to possessions, inability to believe in any reality other than what can be seen and handled, insensitivity and above all, the desire to dominate over other forms of existence, are all signs of the material self gone astray. Skill in manual operations, command of language, emotional stability and quickness of wit as distinct from true intelligence, are marks of the material self in its desirable aspects. You should note that all these good features as well as the bad ones can manifest automatically, that is with the automatic energy (E6).

It would be tempting to say that what I have been describing is nothing but a pattern of conditioned reflexes and not a 'self' at all; but there is certainly more to it than this. The material self can experience pleasure and pain, desire and aversion because the sensitive energy (E5) works in it. It can exercise all the powers of the mind including the creativity that comes from beyond the mind. These actions are possible because the will can be associated with the energies of the material self, and make it into a 'person'. When the will is united with the material self it has no real freedom and is the slave rather than the master of what should be its instrument.

When the material self is permanently dominant, a man becomes a living automaton. He can be very clever and very successful in the material world and gain power over his fellow men by treating them as if they were no more than material objects, but he has no inner life and no possibility of transformation. One cannot help pitying the unfortunate people who have been trapped in their material selves, because they miss all that is most wonderful in human life. Unless something happens to bring them out of the situation, their sole reality will always be the world of lifeless material objects.

The right place of the material self is that of an instrument to be used and controlled by the higher parts of the self. It is right that we should dominate the material world and that we should acquire and enjoy every kind of skill. We should enjoy material objects; but we should never be dependent on them.

Self-observation can teach us to recognize the difference between enjoyment and enslavement. If we find that material objects mean too much to us, we must take steps to destroy our dependence on them.

Some people are quite free from their material selves. I have observed such people with great interest. They have no sense of possession and can give away things and money with no feeling of loss. They usually have a poor contact with their own bodies and are often emotionally unstable. I mention this to bring out the point that it is not enough to be free from material forces: one must have some higher part of the self awake and active to take the place of the material self when this loses its power to dominate us.

Finally, I must say that I disagree with the view that the material self is 'satanical'. This view is held in some religious systems — Christian, Sufi and Buddhist especially. Pak Subuh, for example, calls the material self the Satanical self and the source of all evil in man. It is not the existence of a material self, but its usurpation of the position of Master that is our bane. It can dominate only when it is not observed. The best way of putting it in its right place is to get into the way of noticing how we look at material things and deal with them. If they 'matter' to us, we must be on our guard.

2. The Reactional Self

As the mind-stuff begins to be organized in the young child, it tends to react from the sensitive energy (E5) which is inherently dualistic or polar in character. Like and dislike, pleasure-pain, desire and aversion and all the other 'pairs of opposites' begin to act upon the young mind and produce a second pattern of behaviour. This in the course of a few years — usually between the fourth and seventh years — forms the Reactional Self. This self is connected with the instinctive and emotional centres and it is therefore influenced by heredity. There can be an excessive sensitivity to stimulations of pleasure and pain and this will lead to a dominant Reactional Self. If there is a lack of sensitivity the Reactional Self will be weak.

The pattern of reactions will depend upon the influences that act on the young child. It is closely connected with the personality. It is easy to recognize a man or a woman with dominant reactional self. They will be subject to moods, see everything as 'black or white', be oversensitive to praise and blame. They will have easy enthusiasms and equally easy depressions. When this enthusiasm is uppermost, they have great driving force, but if the material self is weak, they will be unrealistic and impractical.

The reactional self can be inconsiderate, even cruel to others, highly sensitive to its own feelings and unable to feel those of others whom it may wound or offend. It is liable to violent and unreasoning prejudices.

This kind of selfish reactivity is the undesirable aspect of the reactional self. Its good qualities include perceptiveness, love of beauty, capacity for affection and generosity. In the intellectual field, reactional selves are logical, orderly in their mental operations, clear and incisive in expression.

The main value to us of the reactional self lies in its power **to generate force in action.** If we can learn to control its mechanical reactions, the energy that is made available can be used to sustain any required physical or mental activity. When the will is caught into the reactional self, we are dominated by our likes and dislikes and are a nuisance to ourselves and to others. The mind is drawn into the pattern of reactions and we observe such people displaying huge ingenuity in justifying their own prejudices and reactions. If the will withdraws from the reactional self, we can still enjoy vivid experiences of the senses and the mind, but not be lost in or identified with them.

As with the material self, so here also, the reactional self is a bad master, but it can be a good servant.

We should know our reactional self. This means we must observe and remember our likes and dislikes, our prejudices and opinions. This is not an easy task, and it cannot be done by a mental effort alone. It is essential that our will should be engaged, and for this reason, we must set ourselves to struggle with likes and dislikes if we want to know them objectively. One of the most valuable exercises, and one that P. D. Ouspensky regarded as one of the foundations of work on oneself, is the **non-expression of negative emotions.** The reactional self is constantly complaining about trivial ailments and misfortunes, it is jealous, possessive, nervous and unsure of itself; and it expresses all these useless and unnecessary reactions in speech and gesture. The exercise of not showing any of these reactions in our outward behaviour enables us to observe and eventually to control them.

Another very valuable, but easily misunderstood, exercise is that of **non-justifying.** The reactional self hates to be in the wrong: it seeks always to project the causes of its negative reactions outside itself. The mind is diverted from useful activity by the need to explain, to justify, and to present oneself in a good light. As soon as the absurdity and weakness of such a state of affairs becomes obvious, the seeker can set himself to the task of not explaining or justifying his actions. This takes the initiative away from the reactional self and obliges it to accept a subordinate place in the self-hood. There is a pitfall to be avoided, which consists in priding oneself on not justifying and in being 'un-affected by the opinions of others'. I have seen people develop an insufferable superiority, because they have trained themselves never to justify or explain what they do. This is the result of transferring the initiative from the reactional to the divided self (which we shall study in the next section) without understanding the limitations of the divided self.

When the reactional self is well-developed and trained, it makes a very attractive person with a wide range of interests, open and receptive, capable of hard mental or physical work and with a good mind. There is, however, even in the best of cases a tendency to lack discrimination and the power of self-criticism. With normal people, the reactional self is called into activity only when its qualities are needed.

3. The Divided Self

The third self may develop at any time after the tenth year, but I think its natural emergence comes before puberty and the awakening of the sexual powers. It is marked by **the inner sense of right and wrong,** as distinct from the artificial reactions grafted by education on to the reactional self. These artificial reactions may so mask and distort the impulses that come from the conscience that the divided self fails to be organized as an independent seat of the will.

I chose the term **divided self,** which seems to be quite different in meaning from the terms used by the Sufis and others to describe the third state of the soul, to emphasize its two-fold nature. We have two kinds of perception: one through the senses and the associative part of the mind that connects us with the material world and the other through the 'inner sense' (described in section 2 of this chapter) and the **conscience** that connects us with the spiritual world. The commonly quoted saying that man is 'half-animal half-angel' applies to the divided self, but requires serious qualification. The animal — or as I prefer to call it 'lower' — self is human and it knows the world and acts on it in human terms. The angel or spiritual self is far from a perfectly obedient servant of God — as the angels are supposed to be — but simply that part of our nature that is at home in the world of spiritual realities.

We are divided between matter and spirit; but the two parts are not separated. That is why I call it a single self, but divided. This division is one of the basic facts of human existence. If we fail to realize the truth of it, we cannot possibly make any sense of human life. It is very important to pause here and to seriously ask yourself some questions.

First: "Have I a material body and am I connected through it with the material world? Can I picture a state of existence in which I should be what I am, but without a connection with the material world?" You may have some doubt about the last question, but you cannot deny your material existence here and now. The more you reflect on it, the more you will see that it is not possible to think of **human** existence apart from a material body and organs of perception that connect us with the material world.

Second: "Am **I nothing but** the material body and material perceptions? Is my existence neither more nor less than that of tables and chairs, rocks and stones and other material objects? Can I possibly think of myself without my inner experience and all that it implies? Where do my values come from unless from a world that is totally different from the material world?"

These questions must be answered for oneself without looking up books to see what other people have said. One should as far as possible put aside all that one has heard or thought about these things in the past and examine the questions as if one were meeting them for the first time.

What I have just written has a far wider bearing on our search for Truth than simply to clarify our under-

standing of the divided self. One of the hardest requirements of any attempt to deepen our understanding is
to keep an open mind. By this I mean far more than to
put aside prejudice and pre-conceived opinions. **The
mind must take in the question and we must bring to
bear on it all that we know, without allowing ourselves
to have any opinion about it.** We must discover what
presents itself to us, not what we suppose or believe. If
you do this with the question of the divided self I am
sure that you will discover for yourself that you have
the two-fold nature deep down in your mind and that
you cannot argue it out of existence.

The divided self is not just a dumb-bell with two
ends. It is the seat of our character, that is, the essence-
pattern that we were born with, combined with all the
fixations that have developed since childhood and of
which we are usually unaware. Consequently, to know
one's divided self is really to know what kind of a
person one is and what kind of life one should be living.

Unfortunately, we cannot study the divided self by
observation of our mental processes. This is because it
is covered up by the habits of the material and reactional selves; and, in most people, it is scarcely ever
dominant. Nearly all people live almost permanently
on the first two levels of the self-hood and in consequ-
ence their behaviour has little connection with what
they really are. It is, therefore, advisable to leave the
study of the divided self until after having identified
with confidence the content and behaviour pattern of
the lower selves. Once this is done, we begin to see —
almost in spite of ourselves — how we are held, in all
that we do, within the limits of our own character-
pattern.

The divided self is the seat of conscience and discrimination. If we can learn discrimination, we help our divided self to develop in the right way. One mark of the man whose divided self is awake is that he is acutely aware of the duality of his nature. He sees himself drawn powerfully towards both of the two worlds to which he belongs and realizes that he is powerless to reconcile the conflict within his own nature. This awareness is what prepares him for the awakening of his True Self.

4. The True Self

The transformation of **mind** into **soul** is accomplished at the central point of man's being. I call this the True Self, and ascribe to it a triple nature consisting of the natural self, the spiritual self and the individuality. I was led to this conception by Gurdjieff's assertion in *All and Everything* that the true man contains his own law of three-foldness. I believe it is implicit also in the traditional belief that man has a three-fold nature and yet is an individual with a single undivided will. These properties belong to the **True Man,** not to what Gurdjieff called the 'man in quotation marks' which I take to be the man dominated by the lower selves and divorced from his own reality.

I remember being immensely struck thirty or forty years ago when I first read the sermons of Meister Eckhart* at his saying "Man must strive with all his might **to become what he really is."** This paradoxical theme that man has not to become different from what

---

*cf. *Meister Eckhart: A Modern Translation*, Blakney, Harper Torchbooks.

he is, but different from the false man who has usurped the place of the true one, can be understood if we grasp the significance of the four selves.

The True Self should take place at puberty: it is the **seat of conscious creative action** and therefore it should awaken in the sexual act. This is one aspect of the True Self; and it gives the key to understanding what is meant by the 'natural' self.

The higher or spiritual part of the True Self cannot be observed by the mind nor can it even be described because it does not belong to the world of 'name and form'. I can only give my personal belief that the 'higher self' is the pattern of intention or purpose that should guide our lives. This may suggest a kind of blue-print or specification laid down for us by some 'higher power'. In other words, it may seem like predestination. I believe in predestination; not as predetermination in which we have no say, but rather as a decision that we have taken in the very act of entering into existence. It is as if we came into this life to carry out a task that "we" voluntarily accepted before we came. "We" here does not mean our minds, which did not exist at that point; nor does it mean our self, for that also did not exist. It refers to our **will** or our **individuality** which by some act that we cannot picture with our minds, took the decision that committed it to being born as a human being. From this decision came the higher or spiritual part of the self.

I freely admit that this is no more than a personal belief — perhaps no more than an opinion — and it cannot be verified by any means that I can suggest. You can reject it without losing what is important in the notion that at the centre of our being is the True Self that we do not know and that we wish to find. We can use a more concrete picture such as to regard the higher part of the self as the ideal man that we hope to become.

Whatever picture we use, we must avoid ascribing perfection to the higher self. It is limited, incomplete and necessarily imperfect. Moreover it is not the same as "I" or my Individuality. This refers to the third or middle term of the True Self.

The key idea here is that the transformed or perfected man has united the natural and spiritual parts of the self by and through his Individuality. This is the 'Man of the Soul' as Meister Eckhart calls him, and he is able to live in the world of nature as fully and freely as he can in the world of spirits.

There is a great and terrible obstacle in the way of this transformation. This is the **egoism** that has usurped the place of the Individuality. I will say no more about this here as the right place to discuss it will be in the chapter on the liberation of the will.*

I can make one practical suggestion connected with the True Self. This is to set oneself every day to do something creative — something that is an act of one's will and initiative. If we look at our daily lives and make an objective assessment, we shall all of us find that we are carried along by habit and routine — even when we are doing what we should call 'original work'. We do not notice how seldom and how little we do anything that really and truly comes from our own spontaneous choice. Once we can recognize what spontaneity really means, we should open ourselves to such action at least once every day.

---

*Editor's note: This chapter was never written. The reader is referred to *The Dramatic Universe*, Vol III, p. 202 ff.

By doing this, we come a little closer to what we really are. So far as I can discover, the exercise has no harmful consequences unless it is grossly misunderstood. For example, it should be easy to distinguish between spontaneous creative action and the self-will that is determined to have its own way, or the self-indulgence that mistakes licence for creativity. The exercise of creative activity requires of us, in the maximum degree of which we are capable, sincerity, inner freedom and courage. It also calls for a genuine act of will in order to 'make a hole' in our routine activity and find time for spontaneous action. For many years, I have set myself the target of one hour a day allotted to creative work and I have found this very hard to sustain, but very rewarding. Let me add that 'creative work' does not mean only works of genius. Whenever we succeed in emptying our minds of 'intentions', ideas arise spontaneously and we 'see' a creative opportunity opening before us. It is worth while trying to let creativity stir in us, even if for a long time we can make little of it.*

Remember that the purpose of all that I have written in this chapter is to suggest ways in which we can prepare ourselves for transformation by balancing the different parts of our nature and removing obstacles, or at least learning how to surmount them.

5. Rôles — Unconscious and Conscious

Within the framework of the four selves that is common to all human beings, each of us has a set of behaviour-patterns that Gurdjieff called **rôles.** Our rôles determine within very narrow limits the way we

---

*cf. *Creative Thinking*, J. G. Bennett, C.S.P.

act in all kinds of circumstances. No ordinary man or woman is able to behave intentionally by the direction of the mind outside their habitual rôles. This can be verified to a first approximation by noticing how often we rehearse in our minds a new pattern of behaviour, and when the situation actually occurs fall back into our habitual rôle. **We do not speak or act as we intend or wish, but as we are 'wound up to act.'** The point is so important, that we must convince ourselves of it quite beyond doubt. The only way to do this is to set ourselves, as a task, to act a rôle that is quite foreign to us. I will illustrate this by an example that has remained as a vivid memory after nearly thirty years.

Early in the War, in 1940 when travelling was already difficult, I had to go to Glasgow to visit foundries making stoves for air-raid shelters to our design. William R. Gordon, the Director of the Coal Utilization Council, a good friend of mine, asked me to call at his Glasgow office and explain some changes he wished to make. I decided to take this as an opportunity of "playing a strange rôle" by modelling my behaviour in his office upon his own, which I had frequently observed. He was a simple, transparently honest man with great enthusiasm and generosity: but inclined to a loud and dominant manner with his staff. I, on the contrary, was tortuous and indirect in my dealings and inclined to be conciliatory and reluctant to make scenes. As I went up in the lift, I set my face in what I imagined was a fierce expression, stalked angrily into the office and began asking awkward questions. Within thirty seconds, I felt as if I was going to die. I forced myself to continue, but within ten minutes, I had to give up. I made an excuse to telephone and break off the conversation, after which I went back to my habitual behaviour pattern. I tried several times in the following weeks to repeat the experiment, but could not bring myself to do it properly even once. I was really shaken by this demonstration of my own impotence.

I have told this story many times to people who wanted to understand about rôles, but I do not remember a single one who could see why I made such heavy weather of it. This taught me as much as my own experience. Not only are we unable to play any rôles but those that we acquired in childhood, but we cannot even see for ourselves that we are bound hand and foot by our own habitual behavioural patterns.

Psychologists have various ways of describing the commonly occurring rôles, most of which are formed by our relationship with parents, brothers and sisters and the will-patterns of our own character. So much has been written on this subject by Freud, Jung and their followers that it is unnecessary for me to produce yet another scheme.

One vivid and expressive way of distinguishing rôles is to compare them to animals. For some reason we ascribe human features to different species of animals and call people catty, fox-like, tigerish, goat, crocodile or serpent. This language does not properly apply to rôles, but to the dominant feature of a personality. An interesting and useful exercise consists in learning to recognize the different animals in ourselves and in other people.

All exercises of this kind teach us how hard it is to know ourselves and how persistently we close our eyes to our limitations and contradictions. Gurdjieff explained this in a simple way, that agrees with the conclusions of analytical psychology, but is much easier

189

to picture. He said that we are protected from seeing our contradictions by 'buffers' which are formed in the mind during the preparatory age — i.e. up to 18 or 20 years — and as a result of the instinctive impulse to avoid painful or unpleasant experiences. **These buffers are barriers with the mind-stuff that prevent communication between different parts of the personality,** which thus becomes not single but multiple. Instead of the well-defined selves, each operating on its own level, we have a number of separate personalities. In extreme cases, the buffers can be so impenetrable that the personalities are isolated from one another and one of the conditions known as schizophrenia will result. It is often said that one of the tangible aims of therapeutic psychology is to produce integrated personalities. It seldom happens that analytical methods lead to a permanently integrated selfhood and the reason is that buffers are usually too 'solid' to be dissolved by analysis. Violent methods in which the personality is subjected to shock treatment may break down buffers, but if there is no transformation of the selfhood it is most unlikely that an integrated personality will reform from the shattered fragments.

Moderate buffering of the various focal regions of the personality produces stable behaviour patterns and what we call 'normal' people. They are, indeed, normal within the social environment which produced the particular 'buffer-complex' but they quickly get out of their depth if transferred into a different milieu.

As buffers are so important, I shall devote some space to giving illustrations. Buffers are the response of the human mind-stuff to the taboos of the society in which a person develops. In our modern society we have many behavioural taboos. It is not socially acceptable to be in the wrong, and committing mistakes except under duress is taboo. It is not socially acceptable to be seen breaking the rules of the tribe or caste to which we belong. There is therefore the taboo: "thou shalt not be found out."

The taboos act upon every child in the social environment to make it seem necessary to hide defects and mistakes and to justify and explain if one ever is found in the wrong. As, in fact, we know that we make mistakes and do not wish always to keep the rules, we are in a state of self-contradiction that would be hard to bear if we were always conscious of it. We, therefore, begin to hide the truth from ourselves even more assiduously than we do from others. This is not done consciously — it begins in early childhood — and is rather like the way a callus forms to protect damaged tissue. The hardening is in the mind-stuff itself, which in this way develops its buffers.

Buffers which make life easy and enable us to endure with little discomfort the contradictions of the reactional self are an obstacle to the awakening of the True Self. The elimination of buffers must be undertaken with great prudence. I have observed over the years the results of various kinds of shock treatment, and it has seemed to me that these are altogether too risky. Not only can grave harm be done to the personality; but buffers broken down by forceful action are usually soon replaced by other buffers that may be less useful socially and equally obstructive to psychological development. The Pharisaic buffer: "Thank God, I am not as other men", takes many forms. It can appear among those who are on the path of transformation and closes their minds to their own defects. Another buffer is "loyalty". A man may pride himself on his tolerance and broad-mindedness and yet behave in certain circumstances with narrow bigotry. If challenged he will deny intolerance and assert that he prides himself on his loyalty, which compels him to oppose the enemies of the cause he has espoused. This kind of buffer can develop very rapidly, almost to a pathological degree — in people who have been subjected to shock treatment.

A useful exercise is to observe buffers in people we know and give names to them as I have done in the last paragraph. Then we should set ourselves to observe our own behaviour objectively, and try to recognize at least one such buffer in ourselves. At this point, we have to ask ourselves whether or not we sincerely wish to be free from this buffer. One part of our personality will unhesitatingly say: "Yes, I want to face the contradiction and learn to live with it", but another part will not even know that the observation has been made. We have, therefore, to find a way to compel the attention of the buffered part. This can be done by writing the name of the buffer on a sheet of paper and arranging that we shall read it when a different situation arises. For example, if we see that we have the 'loyalty' buffer, we should arrange to be reminded at moments when we are 'doing our duty'.

Sometimes, the absurdity of unnoticed contradictions hits us hard. We see with a sudden shock that we act in ways that are intensely distasteful to our good opinion of ourselves. The force engendered by such involuntary shocks must be turned to good account. We may even ask someone near to us: wife, husband, parent, brother, sister or close friend to remind us when they see us behaving according to the buffered

pattern. We must promise not to react unpleasantly —
we shall do so nevertheless, but the promise will help
to give our friend confidence that we know what we are
asking for — and we must remind ourselves that our
aim is to be free. Freedom is incomparably more
precious than the good opinion of others or our own
self-esteem. Only a great longing for inner freedom will
allow us to bear the suffering that is inevitable when
buffers are removed.

" *When the smallest fragment of Truth enters a
man he can do nothing but obey.* "

THE DRAMATIC UNIVERSE
Volume Three

Claymont Communications was established in 1978 by the Claymont Society to publish and distribute books, tapes and related materials concerning the Work. We carry titles by many authors and offer a wide range of works by J.G. Bennett. For a copy of our latest list write to:

Claymont Communications
P.O. Box 926, Charles Town
W. Va. 25414

THE SEVENFOLD WORK

The Work requires that we try to understand how to work and what the work is for. At the very least it is an action that takes us out of the mechanical stream of events, that demands of us more than animal survival. There are techniques to be learned, ideas to be assimilated and various modes of action to be practiced, but the work is evolutionary and no static set of precepts and exercises can be enough. In this book the work is resolved into a spectrum of seven lines, a truly balanced work, and what belongs to each of the seven lines. It is based on material from talks and discussions held at Sherborne House during 1974.

THE JOHN G. BENNETT TAPES

These tapes hold a message for everyone who believes that our society is approaching a point of crises.

They are cassette recordings of talks given at Sherborne House by John G. Bennett during the five experimental one year courses he conducted there.

In common with many modern thinkers, Bennett believed that man was not fulfilling his obligations to the earth and to his destiny; but unlike many he believed that this could be remedied.

Bennett had a remarkable ability to transmit the most complex ideas in his lectures with conciseness and clarity. His unique way of thinking was often demonstrated in exactly how he said something, as well as in what he said.

Many of the themes are taken from the ideas of G.I. Gurdjieff, expanded and developed by Bennett's own unique and original studies.

A list of these tapes is available from Claymont Communications.

CLAYMONT:
Toward a Working Society

27½ minutes, 16mm, color, sound.

Claymont: Toward a Working Society vividly documents a particular phase in the development of the school and community at Claymont.

The film's fast pace candidly shows many of the diverse aspects of a community striving to achieve a balance between social and family life, obligations to the land, and aspirations towards the higher powers.

Alvin Krinsky's goal of *filming the invisible* is aided by the soundtrack which has recordings of J.G. Bennett, interviews with Claymont residents, and original music composed for the film by Robert Fripp.

Screenings of the film are being arranged by groups in many cities in North America and Europe. Please write to the Film Distributor, Claymont Society, P.O. Box 926, Charles Town, W. Va. 25414 for further information.

THE CLAYMONT SOCIETY

The Claymont Society is based on the ideas of the *Fourth Way*, a term used by Gurdjieff to distinguish a community whose members are working together towards the aim of human transformation within the context of a task to be realized in the world. The task at Claymont itself, is to establish within the next few years a community that will be able to maintain itself under difficult economic and social conditions and to educate people for this purpose.

A necessary task in any community is to achieve unity of purpose and harmony among people of different temperaments and cultural backgrounds. It is above all essential to eliminate the conflicts which come from the desire for power in some and the laziness and self-indulgence in others. Our mutual dependance does not of itself impart any principle of coherence. Our mutual needs do nothing to promote mutual agreement. This can be achieved only if there is a right balance among people at different stages of self perfecting. The society is composed of different groups of members, including candidates of the Basic Course, those who are still training to acquire skills, specialists able to teach and direct activities requiring skill within the context of the spiritual and psychological work, and counsellors able to advise individuals and teach spiritual exercises. When necessary, men and women of exceptional spiritual insight are asked to provide guidance and give new direction to the Society.

The attitude we wish to foster within our society and towards everyone is that we should respect one another.